Choreography

A Basic Approach Using Improvisation

THIRD EDITION

Sandra Cerny Minton, PhD

University of Northern Colorado, Greeley, Emeritus Faculty

Human Kinetics

Library of Congress Cataloging-in-Publication Data

Minton, Sandra Cerny, 1943-
    Choreography : a basic approach using improvisation / Sandra Cerny Minton. — 3rd ed.
        p. cm.
    Includes bibliographical references and index.
    ISBN-13: 978-0-7360-6476-7 (soft cover)
    ISBN-10: 0-7360-6476-1 (soft cover)
1. Choreography. I. Title.
    GV1782.5.M56 2007
    792.8'2—dc22
                    2006103133

ISBN-10: 0-7360-6476-1
ISBN-13: 978-0-7360-6476-7

The Web addresses cited in this text were current as of January 2007, unless otherwise noted.

Acquisitions Editor: Judy Patterson Wright, PhD; **Developmental Editor:** Ragen E. Sanner; **Assistant Editors:** Christine Horger and Anne Rumery; **Copyeditor:** Jan Feeney; **Proofreader:** Joanna Hatzopoulos Portman; **Indexer:** Sharon Duffy; **Permission Manager:** Carly Breeding; **Graphic Designer:** Nancy Rasmus; **Graphic Artist:** Dawn Sills; **Photo Manager:** Laura Fitch; **Cover Designer:** Keith Blomberg; **Photographer (cover):** B & J Creative Photography; **Photographer (interior):** Joe Clithero of B & J Creative Photography, unless otherwise noted; **Art Manager:** Kelly Hendren; **Illustrator:** Ilene Van Gossen (pages 111, 113, 116, 125), Jennifer Delmotte (pages 25, 109, 117), and Al Wilborn (pages 3, 4, 41); **Printer:** Versa Press

Human Kinetics books are available at special discounts for bulk purchase. Special editions or book excerpts can also be created to specification. For details, contact the Special Sales Manager at Human Kinetics.

Printed in the United States of America   10   9   8   7   6   5   4   3   2   1

Human Kinetics
Web site: www.HumanKinetics.com

United States: Human Kinetics
P.O. Box 5076
Champaign, IL 61825-5076
800-747-4457
e-mail: humank@hkusa.com

Canada: Human Kinetics
475 Devonshire Road Unit 100
Windsor, ON N8Y 2L5
800-465-7301 (in Canada only)
e-mail: orders@hkcanada.com

Europe: Human Kinetics
107 Bradford Road
Stanningley
Leeds LS28 6AT, United Kingdom
+44 (0) 113 255 5665
e-mail: hk@hkeurope.com

Australia: Human Kinetics
57A Price Avenue
Lower Mitcham, South Australia 5062
08 8372 0999
e-mail: liaw@hkaustralia.com

New Zealand: Human Kinetics
Division of Sports Distributors NZ Ltd.
P.O. Box 300 226 Albany
North Shore City
Auckland
0064 9 448 1207
e-mail: info@humankinetics.co.nz

To my parents, who made me aware of the value of thinking creatively.
To all the teachers who encouraged my creative ideas.
To my husband, Clarence Colburn, who had infinite patience
during the completion of this and other books.

Contents

Preface

When I first began to study choreography, I was fascinated with many of the dances performed by the professional companies. Each of those works had a unique quality, yet they had a kind of magic and vitality in common. Initially, I thought there was a recipe to be followed that could produce such dances, but later I began to realize no one formula existed with respect to the choreographic process. At best, it is possible to provide some general words and phrases that describe aspects of an effective dance. Eventually, you should come to realize that there are many ways to structure a dance and that producing a successful work depends on how all parts of the work are organized and how they relate to one another and to the audience.

Choreography invites you to share the joys of creating in movement by discovering the infinite variety that can be found within the dance art form when movement is viewed as a medium for artistic expression. At the same time, I hope the information in this book will help you become more aware of the subtleties found in the movements of daily life so you can use those new perceptions to enhance creativity while composing dances. The basic ideas and suggestions provided are adaptable to creative work in different dance forms, and many of the dance concepts can be used for modern, jazz, ballet, and tap dance choreography.

I based this text on my many years of experience in teaching and directing dance. I've used my experiences to help you become comfortable with the creative process of forming movement into dances. This book uses a basic approach and is arranged so that you begin creating by using a discovery process. Whereas the first edition of *Choreography* began with a discussion of form and addressed movement discovery later, with this edition you begin to create with a sense of freedom and without concern for immediately shaping movement into a form.

Improvisation—the key to the choreographic process—is the focus of chapter 1. Improvisation is the ability to explore spontaneously and conceive dance movements that are representative of an idea, a concept, or a dance style. A framework for creating movement and dances has been added to chapter 1 to help you understand the entire dance-making process. Many inspirations are suggested for movement discovery, along with exercises to help you use those inspirations. You'll also find solutions to common problems for beginning choreographers, including the ability to focus, to work through creative blocks, and to learn to remember movement. I hope you can use the information to avoid some of the difficulties that beginners typically experience during the initial stages of creating.

Chapter 2 explains the use of the craft of choreography in designing and shaping the dance. You'll learn how to make more out of less by manipulating and varying the movements you discover through improvisation. Use of stage space is discussed, as is use of the nontraditional choreographic methods of postmodern dance. This edition contains a new section on how various forms of technology can be used in the dance-making process.

In chapter 3 you are given an idea of what to strive for in shaping and forming a dance as well as descriptions of dance forms commonly used by choreographers. In any case, one of the best methods of understanding dance form is to see as much good choreography as possible. Gradually, through observation, you'll begin to discover how to make your own dances and how to apply the concepts presented in this book. One of my former choreography students told me she was very glad I had shown many videos in her class, because it gave her some concrete ideas of how to bring the information presented in this text together with her own creative ideas.

In chapter 4 you are introduced to the steps involved in putting your dance onstage. You will discover the process of holding auditions, creating a rehearsal schedule, choosing and recording accompaniment, designing a lighting scheme, and designing and constructing costumes for your choreography.

You'll find that the chapters are organized similarly. Exercises titled Developing Your Skills allow you to apply the knowledge you've learned from the text. Exercises are arranged from simple to more complex; personal and feeling-oriented experiences are introduced later so that you can gradually gain confidence with creative work. The exercises also appeal to people with a variety of learning styles—visual, auditory, kinesthetic (emphasizing movement), and even tactile (emphasizing sense of touch). You'll note that some of the exercises are intended for one person, whereas others are for groups. If you lead a group through the exercises, remember to choose your words carefully so that your descriptions are precise and movement oriented.

Chapters 3 and 4 include exercises titled Experience in Action, which guide you step by step through the process of observing a finished dance by focusing on specific aspects of the choreographic craft. Each chapter ends with a list of exercises designed to help you organize your own ideas as they relate to the materials presented so that you do creative work first and then perform the movements or dance you have created, and finally you reflect on your creative work. Another new section titled Choreography Challenge concludes each chapter. In this section, you select an inspiration in chapter 1 and then work with that inspiration by creating movements, varying and arranging the movements, and forming them into a dance. By the time you get to the end of chapter 4, you will have created an entire dance for which you will design the costumes, lighting, props, and special effects.

Appendix A contains updated information about sources for dance videos, music copyright, dance floors, and lighting equipment. In appendix B you will find forms to help you assess your finished dance and plan a performance. You can use the form titled Choreographic Assessment Sheet for discussion and comparison of works created by various choreographers. I've found assessment forms helpful. Use of such assessments tends to make choreographic discussion and evaluation more concrete and less subjective. Use the Choreographic Assessment Sheet in appendix B to help you look at your own work as it develops. New to this edition is appendix C, which contains descriptions of dance and technology Web sites. A glossary is also included. To help you identify glossary terms, each term is boldfaced when it is first used in the text.

Although a book is organized in a linear manner, the creative process itself can best be described as circular. As you choreograph, you will probably find that discovery of movement concepts occurs along with forming those materials into a dance. You'll also find that dance making involves a cyclic process in which you return to and repeatedly use the materials presented in the first three chapters of this book. Movements you discover through the creative process will be molded by your knowledge of craft and form so that you gradually refine your raw materials with increased insight to produce a finished dance. This process should become easier with practice and through observation of the choreography of others. Many of the exercises you'll encounter here encourage you to observe finished dances and to keep a journal of your observations. It is also recommended that you keep a journal of all your choreographic ideas and movement materials throughout the dance-making process.

According to Lavender (1996), writing is an important part of learning to choreograph because it causes you to reflect and thus encourages greater perspective and clarity of thought than simply engaging in an impromptu discussion.

The goal of increasing your understanding of the National Dance Content Standards continues to be a goal of the third edition. The seven standards deal with both the technical and creative aspects of dance, outlining what students should know and be able to do as related to each of the standards. The following are the seven National Dance Content Standards (National Dance Association 1996):

1. Identifying and demonstrating movement elements and skills in performing dance
2. Understanding choreographic principles, processes, and structures
3. Understanding dance as a way to create and communicate meaning
4. Applying and demonstrating critical-thinking and creative-thinking skills in dance
5. Demonstrating and understanding dance in various cultures and historical periods
6. Making connections between dance and healthful living
7. Making connections between dance and other disciplines

The National Dance Content Standards are accompanied by a detailed list of achievement standards that are divided into three age-appropriate groups: those for grades K to 4, 5 to 8, and 9 to 12. The publication also contains an appendix of glossary terms and a second appendix of sequential learning experiences for each standard. (You can order your own copy of *National Standards for Dance Education: What Every Young American Should Know and Be Able to Do in Dance* from either the Princeton Book Company at 800-220-7149 or the American Alliance for Health, Physical Education, Recreation and Dance at 800-321-0789.)

Each of the seven standards describes a specific area of dance knowledge or movement skills, but it will be your responsibility, if you become a dance teacher, to bring those standards to life. You can use the achievement standards to design classroom experiences appropriate for the age level, needs, and experiences of your own students. By using the standards as a guide, you should be able to provide meaningful learning experiences in a well-rounded learning environment. Thus, you can use the information in this book in two ways: to improve your present choreographic abilities and as a resource for the future when you might be responsible for teaching the information outlined in the standards.

The concepts presented in this text relate specifically to Dance Content Standards 2, 3, and 4. The dance-making process presented in this book begins with an inspiration. It is possible, however, to use diverse sources as an inspiration. This means ideas, symbols, and stories from other cultures, historical periods, and disciplines can serve as an inspiration, connecting dance making to Dance Content Standards 5 and 7 as well. Use information from the text to increase your understanding of the standards, and then put them into practice by using the explorations, improvisations, and exercises in the chapters.

Acknowledgments

I would like to thank Dan Guyette and Charles Houghton, former University of Northern Colorado faculty, and Brian Garrett and Tim Sutherland, former students, for their advice in preparing the information on lighting in chapter 4. I would also like to thank the five former students, Laurence Curry, Jacob Mora (Artistic Director Mora Por Vida), Jane Sokolik Mora, Tamara Wilkins, and Kaci Wilson, who posed for the studio photographs, and editors Judy Patterson Wright and Ragen Sanner, who encouraged and guided me in writing this third edition.

Exploring and Improvising Movement

I have always found the creative process to be a wonderful yet mystifying experience. It's wonderful because the **dance,** the product, is an entity that can entertain, communicate, and inspire. It's mystifying because through the creative process the **choreographer** is able to energize a previously empty space and make it come alive. With the advent of various computer technologies and the Internet, the possibilities for dance making can be extended and may in the future include not-yet-imagined multimedia forms. Some of the multimedia dance forms combining choreography and technology are described in chapter 2.

Whether a dance includes technological innovations or not, discovering the right movement through improvisation is an important part of the choreographic process. I've noticed that when I felt strongly about improvised movement—when it felt "right"—others felt it was "right" too. Often people would later remark on the section of the dance containing such movements as being appropriate or beautiful or as having meaning.

Chapter 1 explores the goals of the third **Dance Content Standard**—to be able to create and communicate meaning through dance (National Dance Association 1996). This standard is aimed at the initial stages of the choreographic process in which you discover movements that fit a motivating **idea** or express specific meanings. Say you are interested in creating a dance that communicates autumn. To embark on this project, you can read poems about autumn and look at photos taken during the fall season. You can also hike through a park or forest in the fall. All these activities help you focus on your own feelings about autumn. One of my college professors said that autumn reminded her that the year was dying. All of these collected feelings about the fall season make up meanings that are connected to autumn. These are the feelings that you would attempt to communicate through the movements of your dance.

In the beginning, choreographing involves divergent thinking, in which the creative process is important for discovering many possible movement solutions. This chapter begins with an analysis of the creative process and how its stages parallel the steps used in making dances. Suggestions to facilitate creating, such as relaxation and concentration, are also included. Following that discussion are analyses of exploration and improvisation, methods you can use to discover movement, and detailed examples of exploration and improvisation sequences. The chapter concludes with sections on how to meet challenges during the improvisation process, fit movement materials together, and find appropriate music for your dance.

The Creative Process

Choreography is a creative process that requires practice as well as some knowledge of how the process functions. It was once a popular notion that creative work occurred through divine intervention and that only certain people had the capacity to create. Fortunately, today we recognize that although people differ in their capacity to do creative work, anyone can benefit from and enjoy being creative. The task is not easy, but having a knowledge of creative problem-solving strategies should enable you to work through blocks that surface during your choreographic efforts.

There are five steps, or stages, in the creative process (Csikszentmihalyi 1997):

1. A period of preparation
2. Time for incubation
3. Occurrence of insight
4. Sessions in which evaluation occurs
5. A period of elaboration

During the **preparation** phase, the person doing the creating gets immersed or involved in the topic in a way that arouses interest or curiosity. Immersion in a topic can be both a conscious and unconscious process. During **incubation,** ideas churn in the creator's unconscious mind—a process that often gives birth to insights. In the end, the person doing the creating must decide whether the insights are valuable and whether they should be expanded.

Choreography has its own stages of creating. The important part about choreographing, however, is that these stages are fluid and can and should be revisited often so that the dance becomes an ever-evolving creative effort. In dance terms, one could say that a dance evolves through the following processes:

1. Observation of an inspiration: The choreographer notices something, such as an object, idea, or event that inspires an idea for a dance. Anything can spark an inspiration, even works of art, poetry, or music.

2. Feeling response: The choreographer feels a **response** to that inspiration that he or she would like to portray through the dance.

3. Memories + imagination = movement: The choreographer pulls from memories and imagination to help improvise movements to be used in the dance.

4. Dance + visual design: The choreographer enhances the dance with elements of visual design, such as costumes, lighting choices, props, and technology, although sometimes technology is an integral part of creating movements early on.

Figure 1.1 is a visual framework for the creative movement and dance-making process as discussed in this book. In this framework, the choreographer must first carefully **observe** his or her inspiration for a dance. Robert and Michele Root-Bernstein (1999) have written extensively about how highly creative people think, noting that active observation, or taking the time to look repeatedly, is a trait of great artists. After observing, the choreographer has feelings about or a response to the inspiration. This response is, in turn, combined with images and memories and transformed into movement. Later, these movements can be modified and molded into a dance that can be performed, understood, and appreciated.

The only thing wrong with the creative dance-making process is that the process is not linear as depicted in the diagram. Instead, the person doing the creating moves back and forth within the process so that elaboration or variation of movement is frequently interrupted by periods of incubation, added insights, observations, and further analysis of one's response. New feelings arise, suggesting new directions for the work being created (Csikszentmihalyi 1997). In choreographic terms, the person making the dance may have added feelings concerning the inspiration that give rise to new movement insights, causing the dance to take on a different direction or form. Thus, a more realistic model of the framework for movement discovery and dance making is the one shown in figure 1.2. The first three steps of the choreographic

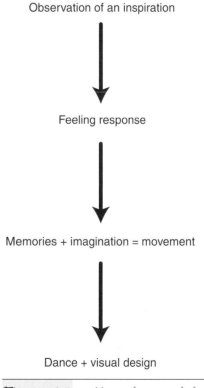

Observation of an inspiration

Feeling response

Memories + imagination = movement

Dance + visual design

Figure 1.1   Linear framework for the creative movement process.

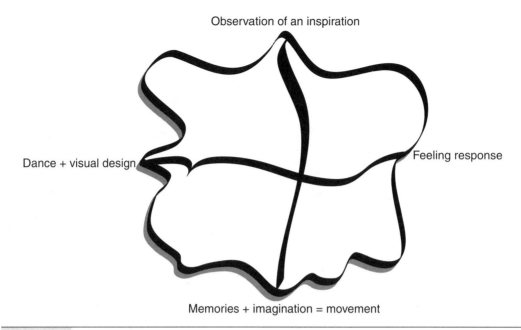

Observation of an inspiration

Feeling response

Dance + visual design

Memories + imagination = movement

Figure 1.2 This model for the creative movement framework is more realistic than the linear framework because it allows for the more circular process necessary for creating original dances.

process—observation of an inspiration, feeling response, memories + imagination = movement—are discussed in this chapter. The final step—dance + costumes and lighting—is discussed in chapters 2, 3, and 4.

Observation and Feeling Response

Before you begin to choreograph, you need to discover the **inspiration,** or intent, that will guide you through the dance-making process. As a choreographer, you must observe this inspiration and have a feeling response to it. This is also when you set the creative task and decide on the scope, extent, and dimensions of the problem to be solved. This first step in the choreographic process is part of the preparation stage of the creative process, and at this point you are free to select one of many inspirations. For example, if you decide to create a dance based on a painting, you will need to observe the painting from multiple viewpoints and assess your feelings about the painting. The problem to be solved is to capture your observations and feelings about the painting in movement. If you choose to choreograph to a specific piece of music, the creative problem to be solved is to observe or immerse yourself in the music and find movements that capture your feeling response to the score as well as correctly interpret the various qualities and dynamics of the musical score. A piece of choreography based on human gestures would involve observing and exploring the selected gestures and then varying those gestures. Likewise, a dance growing from an emotional base would involve observing or investigating the nuances of those feelings. While the choreographer can alter the scope or nature of a dance at a later stage, you must have an inspiration or place from which to begin. Preparation also generally involves gathering your resources together so that you may begin.

Inspirations can be visual, auditory, tactile, or kinesthetic. Various types of **props** and imagery can also be used to facilitate improvisational experiences. Examples of each type of inspiration and motivation follow.

Inspirations and Motivations

1. Visual
   - Pictures from magazines and books
   - Colored paper cut into different shapes
   - Various kinds of line patterns such as scallops, zigzags, spirals, or a combination of these
   - Interesting natural objects, such as shells, pinecones, leaves, or starfish
2. Auditory
   - Recorded music, particularly modern or **electronic music**
   - Music played live in the dance studio on drums, cymbals, bells, tambourines, or any other instrument
   - Body sounds, such as slapping, clapping, snapping the fingers, or stamping the feet
   - **Rhythmic patterns** made with the body by slapping, clapping, and so on
   - Vocal sounds such as hissing, clacking the tongue, or whistling
   - Nonsense syllables, words, or even poetry or prose phrases
   - Words with **kinesthetic** qualities, such as *ooze, melt, soar, collapse,* or *dart* (Ellfeldt 1967)
3. Tactile
   - Objects with interesting qualities to the touch, such as furry, slimy, slippery, sharp, or soft
   - Natural objects with interesting tactile qualities
   - Objects providing for tactile and spatial explorations, such as a chair, the inside of a large box, or a corner of the dance studio
4. Kinesthetic
   - Pedestrian movements from daily life, including walking, running, lifting, and falling
   - Waving, saluting, shaking hands, and other gestures from life experiences
   - **Axial** (also known as nonlocomotor) movements, such as reaching, stretching, pushing, pulling, swinging, swaying, bending, straightening, and turning in place
   - **Locomotor** movements from technique class, such as running, hopping, jumping, leaping, skipping, sliding, galloping, and turning
   - **Combinations** of movements from dance technique classes
   - **Paths,** or **pathways,** traced on the floor or in the space around the body
   - Writing words or names in space or as a **floor pattern**
5. Props
   - Various pieces of clothing pulled from the costume closet or brought from home, including capes and skirts of various lengths and fullness
   - Pieces of material draped on the body in a variety of ways
   - Hoops of various colors
   - Scooters used in children's physical education classes
   - Sticks and poles of varying lengths and thickness (see figure 1.3)
   - Elastic bands that stretch in many directions (see figure 1.4); the elastic bands need to be at least two inches wide and long enough to form a loop to surround a dancer's body

- Elasticized sacks covering the body (see figure 1.5); such sacks can be pushed or extended into a variety of shapes
- Scarves and streamers of various lengths to create designs in space as a dancer moves

6. Multimedia
   - Slides
   - PowerPoint projections
   - Computer graphic projections
   - Video projections
   - Projected images based on motion capture
   - Images transmitted via the Internet

7. Imagery
   - Scenery, such as mountains, lakes, and plains

Figure 1.3 The dancers are using a scooter and sticks as props.

From The New York Public Library for the Performing Arts, Jerome Robbins Dance Division, Astor, Lenox and Tilden Foundations.

Figure 1.4 Use of elasticized bands to create designs in space. Nikolais Dance Theatre performing *Tensile Involvement*.

Figure 1.5 An example of a sack-like costume that can be pulled and stretched in many directions. Nikolais Dance Theatre in Group Dance from *Sanctum*.

- Body feelings, which can include the feeling of lying on a warm, comfortable mattress or of having your feet on a hot sidewalk
- Dramatic situations, such as pretending that you're being chased by someone or that you're finding your way across a darkened room
- Unusual **environments,** such as the inside of a block of Swiss cheese or the inside of a piano (Hanstein 1980)

Imagery depends on memories and past experiences, and dancers are able to use various images as inspiration by relating the image to their memories. Thus, imagery used for improvisation should be meaningful for those involved in the improvisation. If you have spent very little time in the mountains or at the beach, for example, it would be difficult to relate to those images. Instead, choose images that come from your own experiences. I grew up in the Chicago area. My family and I frequently spent weekend days at the sand dunes on the southern shore of Lake Michigan. I can still see images in my mind: waves lapping at the shore, the color and texture of the sand, and dull green vegetation that grew higher up on the dunes. I also remember the texture and taste of the sandwiches we ate while seated on a blanket, the prickly sizzle of the hot noonday sand against my bare feet, and the feeling of relaxation that permeated such a day.

Images can also be quite varied. Select motivating images that are easy to use and that suit the way in which you learn. For example, use **visual images** if you like pictures or diagrams, and use **kinesthetic images** if you find it easy to tune in to bodily feelings. Keep in mind that visual and kinesthetic are only two kinds of imagery; table 1.1 provides a more detailed explanation of the various forms imagery can take.

To a choreographer, preparation means several things. First, the process of creating a dance means developing a sensitivity to and awareness of your body so that you are able to connect with and act on **impulses** for movement. Movement impulses are connected with the inspiration for your creative work.

Keep in mind that the ability to tune in to bodily movements is not the same as having a high level of dance **technique.** It has more to do with being aware of the kinesthetic feelings and visual images associated with each movement or movement **phrase.** Dancers who have

Table 1.1 Types of Imagery

Type of imagery	Definition	Example
Visual[a]	A picture in the mind.	Visualize your body as a star.
Kinesthetic[a]	Body feelings. What the body should feel.	Imagine the feeling of your feet on a hot sidewalk.
Direct[b]	Similar to mental rehearsal or seeing specific movements in your mind.	Visualize yourself performing a leap.
Indirect[c]	A metaphor for the movement. Exists outside your body.	Move like a dry leaf as it floats to the ground.
Specific[d]	An image directed to a particular part of the body.	Lift one arm and focus on the feeling of heaviness in that arm.
Global[d]	General images that include the entire body.	Imagine your whole body as transparent.

[a]Paivio 1971.
[b]Overby 1990.
[c]Studd 1983.
[d]Hanrahan and Salmela 1990.

a heightened body awareness have a command and versatility of movement—an ability different from having advanced technique. Technique itself can get in the way of creating because it can cause the choreographer to think in terms of steps rather than discover new movements from a fresh viewpoint. Although creating a dance using steps such as pas de bourrée from ballet or a time step from tap dance is possible and appropriate at times, you should go beyond set steps to discover unique movements and arrangements of movements that fit the intent of a dance. For example, set steps could be used in a dance representing a historical period or a specific dance form such as ballet, but you are still encouraged to explore your creativity in such contexts. You can also use set steps as a starting point by varying them through the use of movement explorations described later in this book.

Choreographic preparation also involves learning about the **craft** of choreography. Craft involves elements such as these:

- Understanding the use of **stage space**
- Working with the relationship between dancers
- Using movement variation and **manipulation**

Choreographic craft is explained in chapters 2 and 3. The important point is to use your understanding of the choreographic craft so that craft does not get in the way of creating. If you rely solely on the craft, you will have problems discovering innovative ways of moving.

Researching Your Ideas

Research is another aspect of preparing to choreograph a dance. Choreographic research can take many forms:

- Analyzing your accompaniment for a thorough knowledge of musical form, development, and qualities of feeling
- Understanding your dancers' movement styles and capabilities
- Studying background information on the **subject matter** of your dance

- Learning about the philosophy of a historical period
- Comparing elements of **design** used in movements in the arts, such as **realism, cubism, and expressionism.**

Through research, the choreographer finds a nucleus from which creating can begin and from which it can continue to develop.

Developing Your Skills

CHOREOGRAPHIC RESEARCH

1. If your choreographic inspiration is a piece of music, try to gain a thorough understanding of your accompaniment. Listen to your music many times before you begin the movement discovery process. Understand the metric structure and notice where one section of the music ends and another begins. Pay specific attention to how the composer has developed the score. For example, does the music build to a high point and then come to an abrupt conclusion, or does it build and then end gradually? Be aware of changes in the feelings evoked by the music as well.

2. Determine whether the music is suitable for the **style** of your proposed choreography. To determine whether the accompaniment is appropriate, you will need to be very clear about the intent and proposed style of your dance, and you will need to choose music that matches the tone and quality of your movement. Soft, flowing music usually is used to accompany soft, flowing (lyrical) movement, whereas a percussion score complements movement performed in a percussive style. But you might want to choose music that contrasts in style or tone with your choreography. Such an approach could highlight the style of the movements in your dance or, when taken to an extreme, could be comical.

3. Many dances include specific characters or a progression of events. Listen to the music to determine whether the musical form and development fit the visualized development of your dance.

4. Take time to watch your dancers move in class or in an improvisation session. Observe such elements as the dancers' preferred movement style and the specific movements in which each is particularly skilled.

5. After analyzing how your dancers move, visualize the point in your choreography where specific dancers might best be included or which dancers should perform a particular role.

6. Decide if you can showcase specific dancers' abilities in one or more parts of your dance. You might even want to make a portion of the dance an elaboration of a dancer's talents.

7. Keep a journal (a written record) of the metric organization and dynamic changes of your accompaniment, the possible relationship between musical progression and the visualized development of your dance, and the movement strengths of your dancers. In some instances you might prefer to use drawings or diagrams to help you remember movements, relationships among dancers, and other moments of inspiration. Keeping a record of your ideas will help you recall them at later choreographic sessions.

8. Another form of choreographic preparation or research is to review background material on the subject matter of your choreography. These materials might include the following:

- Historical events or episodes
- Information about well-known personalities
- Stories or myths associated with a specific cultural group
- Descriptions of important artistic trends or movements, such as the blues in music, impressionism in the visual arts, or the dance forms of the ancient Greeks

9. When researching background materials, take detailed notes. Later you can review them to determine which elements can be adapted most easily to a movement format. You'll find it very helpful to condense your notes and group together the elements and ideas that relate to the same character or event.

10. Finally, you might want to research various forms of media and computer technology to determine whether any of them could contribute to the tone or style of your work. For example, in a dance based on historical events, you could project images from the historical period on the backdrop. You could also project computer-generated images or word phrases that highlight the message of your work.

Allowing Ideas to Incubate

As you work through the choreographic process, you will find that it can be punctuated by periods of incubation, when you put aside the work you're creating to allow you to test and perhaps gain some understanding of aspects of the work. Putting your dance aside allows your subconscious to go to work. Such periods of incubation can be especially helpful when you reach points during which you feel blocked. I have always been amazed with the process of incubation because when I return to a creative project a day or two later, new movement ideas seem to spring forth. My guess is that the period of incubation allows for a change in perspective, which allows for renewed creativity. Later you can shape movement into a **composition** using your knowledge of the choreographic craft.

Having Movement Insights

The third step in the creative movement framework—memories + imagination = movement—is the focus of the rest of this chapter and the step most people relate to original artistic work. In terms of the framework for creating movement and dance making, we deal with movement discovery, or insights, in the remainder of this chapter. In choreography the initial part of the creative act is the discovery of movement for your dance. It is in this step that you generate movement ideas and possibilities.

Appropriate movement is usually discovered through **improvisation.** During improvisation, the choreographer moves spontaneously while concentrating on the inspiration for or intent of the work. In some situations, the dancers improvise using suggestions made by the choreographer, and the choreographer then decides which movements or phrases will be included in the dance.

Before moving on to discussions of exploration and improvisation, you should become familiar with the benefits of concentration and relaxation as a part of the creative process.

Concentrating and Relaxing

As a beginning choreographer, you can do many things to refine your creativity. The first of these is to strengthen the connection between your mind and body by developing your ability to concentrate. Through better concentration, you will be able to identify and recall movements that come to you during the improvisational process because you will learn to dance and create from the inside.

Lorna Marshall (2002), an instructor at the Royal Academy of Dramatic Arts in London, wrote that in any type of performance it is essential to get your attention fully integrated with your body. Being able to do this means getting rid of habitual movements and postures and listening to what is happening in your body moment by moment. In an improvisational setting, this means that you should learn to focus on the kinesthetic feeling of each movement and any accompanying visual **images** that arise while still being aware of your surroundings and other dancers sharing your space.

Concentration is enhanced by the ability to relax, allowing you to be more receptive to **movement ideas** and images as they come forth. Eric Maisel (1995), a psychotherapist who has worked with artists and performers, describes several relaxation exercises to help people deal with anxieties that arise while doing creative work. One technique is to exhale slowly until your lungs feel completely empty, and then let the inhalation phase of breathing take care of itself. Another technique is to imagine that your arms and legs have become heavy, then visualize tension flowing out of your body by exiting through your fingertips. David Ulrich (2002), who has studied many types of creative people, recommends stepping back from the creative process from time to time by assuming a state of active stillness. Ulrich recommends learning how to meditate in order to attain this state.

Popular courses in stress reduction employ relaxation techniques. Many years ago, Edmund Jacobson created a system called progressive relaxation, which enables a person to identify points of tension in the body by distinguishing them from relaxation in the same body part. The reasoning is that people who have little or no sensitivity to body tension allow these tensions to accumulate, and over time the body becomes accustomed to the tensions, unaware of their building intensity. An updated version of Jacobson's method involves tensing a body part, such as the hand, by making a fist and noticing the tension in the forearm. After consciously experiencing the muscular tension, you release the tension and compare the tense state to the feeling of looseness that accompanies relaxation (Robertson 2000).

Authorities on creative work discuss a state of mind that tends to be compatible with successful creative problem solving. This state is between the conscious and the subconscious and one in which daydreaming takes place. In his book *Imagination*, Harold Rugg (1963) notes that creating requires one to find the threshold level of a mental state in which the mind is off guard, relaxed, and receiving messages or ideas related to the creative work at hand. In other words, you need to arrive at a mind–body condition in which your mind hovers between conscious and subconscious states and in which your body is fairly relaxed. Total relaxation, however, is not appropriate, since creative work requires a sufficient amount of tension or anxiety to keep the creative act moving forward. Psychologist Mary-Elaine Jacobsen (1999) states that when you are engaged in creative work, you need to maintain a state of balance. This means being exhilarated while avoiding the two extremes of behavior in which you are totally wired or completely listless.

Mental images can be helpful for achieving a balanced state of the body necessary for doing creative work. Mirka Knaster (1996), a massage therapist, describes how imagery is used by practitioners of ideokinesis to achieve a more balanced body. In this system, the person imagines lines of movement designed to bring the various segments of the body (head, spine, rib cage) closer to the body's line of gravity so that muscles no longer need to strain to maintain alignment. According to Martin Rossman and David Bresler (2004), cofounders of the Academy for Guided Imagery, imagery can even help solve psychological problems and influence the autonomic nervous system in a way that aids physical healing. When launching into creative work, you might find it helpful to focus on the image of lines of movement bringing body segments closer to the body's line of gravity or other images you find useful to achieve a balanced state of mind and body. Without such a balanced state, the connection between mind and body can be blocked by excess tension and feelings of anxiety. In fact, any type of work involving solving a problem in a creative way is nearly impossible in the face of excessive tension.

Dancers can improve concentration and the **mind–body connection** by learning to pay attention to bodily sensations. You can begin to develop your ability to concentrate during **technique classes.** While you are in these classes, do not allow your mind to wander; if you find this happening, pull your mind back to the body level. At the same time, try to remain as relaxed as possible while still maintaining your concentration.

Developing Your Skills

CONCENTRATION AND RELAXATION

1. To learn to recognize muscular tension, lie on the floor in a comfortable position with your legs straight and your arms at your sides. (You may want to cushion your body by lying on a mat.) Focus your attention on one arm, making it as tight and as tense as possible. Your arm should feel tense, and your hand should make a fist. Now, beginning with your fingers, relax your hand so that the sensation of relaxation flows inward toward the center of your body. Distinguish tension from relaxation by tuning in to the kinesthetic feelings associated with the two different states. Try tensing and relaxing other body parts. Finally, tense the whole body, and then initiate relaxation by beginning at the periphery of the body.

2. Relaxed breathing can be practiced in almost any body position. For this exploration, again lie on the floor with your legs straight and your arms at your sides. Begin by taking several deep breaths. Imagine that your lungs are two balloons or sacks, and **visualize** those two sacks filling as you inhale and emptying completely as you exhale.

3. Another relaxation exercise consists of breathing into different parts of your body. Focus your breathing in your center, and then as you continue to breathe, see your breath extend into other parts of your body as it flows outward. Make a special effort to direct your breath into tense places in your body.

4. Try breathing in different directions as well so that your breath flows horizontally and vertically through your body.

5. Attempt to breathe all the way down to your pelvic floor and up through the top of your head.

6. Many mental images encourage relaxation. For example, imagine that you are lying on a featherbed or on a beach on a warm day, or see your body floating above the ground. Create some of your own images. Select a relaxing image, focus on it, and see it in your mind. (You can improve your **focus** by closing your eyes.)

7. Samuels and Bennett (1973) describe the following exercise that combines breathing with the use of imagery. Take several slow and deep breaths from the abdomen. With each exhalation, imagine that you are taking energy from the universe to become more relaxed; see the inside of your body growing brighter and more radiant from the center outward. This exercise is designed to produce relaxation and increase energy.

8. You can use time in technique class to learn how to focus on sensations that arise from your body. Begin by identifying the kinesthetic sensations that accompany specific technical exercises. For example, feel the widening and narrowing of the plié, the abrupt flatness of the flexed foot; the roundness of second-position

arms; or the spreading of the toes when the foot is flat on the floor. Also, you'll find technique class becomes more interesting if you can concentrate on such kinesthetic sensations or images.

Discovering Movement Through Exploration

One way to develop competence in dance improvisation is to begin with movement **exploration.** Like improvisation, movement exploration is spontaneous, and the movements that come forth are unplanned. The process of exploration, however, is guided largely by suggestions that produce fairly brief movements, whereas improvisation is a much longer and more involved process. Exploration is usually guided very closely by your teacher's or your own use of more superficial **motivations,** or **stimuli,** such as brief spoken suggestions for movement. Improvisation, on the other hand, begins with an inspiration, but it continues because the creator is stimulated by more personal and internally oriented **cues** (Hawkins 1988). During improvisation, the inspiration serves mainly as a point from which you begin moving. You continue to improvise by drawing on your own inner cues and images. (See table 1.2 for examples of movement exploration and improvisation.)

Table 1.2 Examples of Exploration and Improvisation

Motivation or Inspiration	Exploration	Improvisation
Direction	Move one arm in front, behind, to the side, and in diagonal directions in relation to your body.	Begin by moving one arm in different directions. As you move your arm, let your body follow in that direction. Try moving other body parts, letting your body follow those parts as well.
Shapes	Move one arm in a geometric shape, such as a circle. Trace this same shape with other parts of your body.	Begin by moving one arm in a circle. Try moving other parts of your body in a circle. Change the size of the circles, and then move through space as you continue to trace circles with different parts of your body.
Gravity	Lift one arm to the side of your body. As gravity pulls down on your arm, let it get heavy and move downward in response. Do this exercise slowly.	Begin by lifting one arm and lowering it in response to the pull of gravity. Try lifting and lowering other parts of your body. Continue to concentrate on the heavy feeling created by gravity. Slowly lower and lift your entire body. Practice lifting and lowering different parts of your body while you move through space.
Mirroring	Stand and face your partner. The leader begins to move by exploring the potential for movement at different joints. The other person mirrors the movements of the leader. Do this exercise slowly.	Stand and face your partner. The leader does a short movement and stops. This movement should be motivated by a specific idea, image, or feeling. When the leader stops, the other dancer moves in reaction to the leader's movement.

Movement exploration and improvisation can also be explained in terms of the **framework** introduced in figures 1.1 and 1.2. In exploration, the mover must carefully observe the motivation, whether it be in the form of words or a part of the body. In some instances, the person doing the exploring may even have a feeling response to the motivation. Improvisation, however, is a deeper and more personal process such that observing and responding are followed by imagining and remembering. In both processes—exploration and improvisation—the observations and responses are transformed into movement nonetheless.

You can begin exploration experiences with motivations based on the body's movement possibilities or other simple movement ideas. Novice dancers find that such motivations are concrete and easy to use. Following are some specific examples of movement exploration experiences. You may want to try some of these exercises with your eyes closed to heighten your ability to concentrate on body sensations; when possible, focus on both the visual and kinesthetic aspects associated with each suggestion. As you begin to move, see an image in your mind while you concentrate on the resulting kinesthetic sensations in your body.

Developing Your Skills

MOVEMENT EXPLORATIONS

Seated Explorations

All of the following explorations take place in a seated position. Use the tailor position (with the legs folded and crossed, knees out to the side) unless it is uncomfortable. As you perform these seated and standing explorations, practice observation by tuning in to the body feelings you experience. Your response is your movement response to the exploration.

1. Focus on your right shoulder. Lift your shoulder up toward your ear. Lower your shoulder to a centered position and immediately press it to the back. Return your shoulder to the center and then lower it. Finally, after returning your shoulder to the center, press it forward and then return it to the center. Use the shoulder to connect each of these **directions**—up, back, down, and forward—with a continuous circle. Try circling your shoulder in both forward and backward directions.

2. Employ the same type of exploration in the upper body that you used for the shoulder so that you take the upper body forward, to the side, back, and to the other side. End this exploration by circling the upper body from the waist.

3. Explore the possible movements in the various joints of your arm. Notice that the shoulder has a greater **potential** for movement than the elbow. See how many different ways each joint in the arm moves.

4. Concentrate on your right arm, and allow it to begin to move in space. Try moving your arm in different directions and at different **levels** in relation to your body.

5. Lift your arm to the side of your body and trace a shape, such as a circle. Use your arm to trace other shapes, such as triangles or zigzag lines.

6. Concentrate on connecting the **flow** of **energy** from your torso with the energy in your arm. Alma Hawkins (1988) suggests that there is a tensional relationship between the extremities and the center of the body. You can feel this relationship kinesthetically by allowing energy to flow back and forth between the center and periphery of your body. See the ebb and flow of energy in your mind while you feel the energy expand and shrink in your body. Then let the flow of energy move your arm in space. Try this exercise with other body parts.

Standing Explorations

1. Hawkins (1988) points out that dancers must contend with gravity at all times. You can use the pull of gravity to motivate an exploration. Start from a position in which you are sitting on the floor and are relatively relaxed. Allow your body to begin lifting very slowly off the floor and gradually come to a standing position. Concentrate on the feeling of heaviness as gravity pulls down on all parts of your body. Feel gravity's pull and heaviness as you rise. Sense your body growing taller as you lift off the floor. When you reach as tall as you can, descend slowly back to the floor. Be aware of body tension and the pull of gravity throughout the whole standing and sitting process.

2. As a variation, remain standing and lift one part of your body away from the floor, focusing on gravity as it pulls down on that body part. As the body part grows heavier, allow it to give in to gravity.

3. As you stand, allow yourself to slump forward from the waist, and then slowly uncurl the body to a tall standing position. Try this slumping and uncurling action at a fast, medium, and slow tempo. Perform the same action intermittently rather than continuously so that the movement proceeds in a stop-and-start manner. Explore other torso movements, such as stretching up, reaching diagonally, or twisting, but continue to concentrate on the kinesthetic feeling of each of these actions.

4. Concentrate on your right arm, and allow an impulse of energy to move it. Try applying different amounts of energy to your arm, and notice where and how far your arm travels in space. Be sensitive to tensions and muscular feelings associated with a varied use of energy. Do this exploration in another part of your body.

5. Pick a simple movement such as reaching, and try it with one arm. Make this movement as large as possible, and then see how small you can make the same movement. Finally, choose a **size** for your reach that falls between large and small. See if you can change the size of that movement without stopping. Try this exploration with other body parts and with other movements.

6. Rest quietly in a well-aligned stance. Be aware of the swaying of your body as you maintain a normal standing position. Increase the swaying of your body to see how much you can sway before you go off balance.

7. Throw your hips to one side so that they extend beyond your base. **Experiment** by shifting your hips forward, backward, to the side, and in diagonal directions. Determine how far you can shift your hips before you fall. According to Hawkins (1988), you maintain balance by shifting your hips in one direction and your upper body in another. Play with being on and off balance. Then allow yourself to shift so much that you must take some steps in order to realign and center your body. Experiment with losing and recovering your balance as you move across the dance space.

8. Move slowly around the dance space, and be aware of how your total **alignment** tilts forward as you move. You'll find that maintaining good posture is more difficult while you're moving. Practice changing the degree of tilt in your whole body as you move, and then shift a single part of your body out of line while you're moving and see what happens. Change the speed of your locomotion from slow to fast and back to slow again to see how it affects your alignment and ability to travel across space.

9. In another exploration, you can experiment with various uses of **space** or **time.** This exercise begins by moving on a basic **pulse,** also known as the beat. You can supply the pulse by playing recorded music or by beating on a drum. Try changing the level or direction of your movements every eight **counts,** every four counts, and then every two counts. Next, try making changes in the **tempo** of your movements at similar intervals, or hold a position for a certain number of counts before continuing with your movement.

Partner Explorations

For this set of explorations, **following** and **mirroring,** you need a partner or partners. Following and mirroring allow you to enjoy exploration experiences while developing your ability to perceive the movement of another person (see figures 1.6 and 1.7). Throughout these explorations, remember that the dancer who is the leader initiates the movement, and the follower must see those movements and duplicate them. Leaders can easily find movements by exploring the **movement potential** of various parts of the body. Keep your movements slow, short, and simple in both following and mirroring exercises. If you are following, do not try to anticipate the leader's actions; rather, experience movement as it happens. You can practice observing by looking at details of the movements demonstrated by the leader, such as direction, level, position, pathway, quality, rhythm, size, and timing, while your response is again your movement response.

1. Stand behind another dancer, and attempt to follow and replicate the lead dancer's actions. Be aware of the **shape,** flow, and direction of your leader's movements. If you are the leader you may be most comfortable by beginning to move a single

Figure 1.6 The dancers closer to the camera are following the movements of the dancer who is farther way.

Figure 1.7 Mirroring in which one dancer is facing the other.

body part. Later, let your movement extend into other parts of your body. Attempt to connect one body shape to the next by being sensitive to energy flow and impulses.

2. Mirroring is done while **facing** another person. In mirroring, one person is again designated as the leader and the other person attempts to mirror the leader's movements. When the leader moves on the right side, the person following does the same action on the left. It is also necessary for the leader to remain facing the partner while moving, since turning back to back destroys concentration. To begin, the leader can again explore the movement potential of various joints.

Figure 1.8 The dancers are doing an exploration in which three of those involved follow the movements of the dancer located at the front point of the square.

3. The next exercise is for a group of four. Begin by standing in the shape of a square. (Each dancer stands on one corner of a square, and all face the same direction, with the leader positioned in front of other group members, as shown in figure 1.8.) As the leader begins to move, the other dancers in the square follow the movements. At some point, the leader gives his or her role to another dancer by turning toward or extending the gestures toward that group member. The second dancer then assumes the leadership role without allowing a pause or break in group momentum.

4. Mirror the movements of another dancer after he or she has done each movement. (The leader's movement sequences need to be short so that the person following can remember all the actions and thus move after, rather than simultaneously with, the leader.) Continue by mirroring the leader's movements each time the leader stops.

5. Stand facing your partner. After the leader has done a short movement, attempt to move in a direction opposite to the direction of the leader's action. Continue moving by choosing actions that are opposite to the direction of the leader's movements, but try not to change any other aspects of the leader's actions.

6. Partner explorations can also be performed with projected images. For example, you can follow or mirror the movements of a figure projected on a large screen. You could even attempt to create movements that reflect the emotions communicated by projected figures or by projected facial expressions.

Discovering Movement Through Improvisation

Appropriate movement for a dance is usually discovered through improvisation. During improvisation, the choreographer moves spontaneously while concentrating on or observing the inspiration for the work. In Hawkins' (1988) view, the choreographer is guided in improvisation by the initial inspiration selected for composing a dance. In some situations, the dancers improvise by using suggestions made by the choreographer, and then the choreographer decides which movements or phrases will be included in the dance.

Improvisation is a more complete and internally motivated experience than exploration because the choreographer uses his or her feeling response to the inspiration as part of the motivation for movement. In improvisation, the creator also has a hand in selecting the inspiration for movement, or at least part of the inspiration, because it's necessary to relate to the inspiration by using memories and experiences for continued action. Improvisation also provides more opportunities to vary movement and get involved in the process of feeling and forming. It is during the feeling and forming phase of improvisation that **transforming** takes place, as well, since the inspiration becomes movements that can be shaped into a dance. The Root-Bernsteins (1999) state that transformation takes place when creative people use one set of thinking tools to define a problem, a second set to investigate it, and a third set to solve the problem. In the language of dance, this statement means the inspiration may be a painting (visual), but it can be analyzed and appreciated in terms of its rhythmic use of line (**auditory**) and textures (**tactile**) that play across its surface. Finally, the problem to be solved is to create a movement (kinesthetic) interpretation of the painting.

While you improvise, be aware of how your movements connect and develop, and notice the beginning, middle, and end of your actions. When you have discovered many possibilities, find a **closure** for your movement by letting the ending develop naturally. Hawkins (1988) also contends that a successful improvisation should leave the person with a feeling of unity, satisfaction, and fulfillment. The Root-Bernsteins (1999) believe that because transformations are not really equal in terms of the thinking tools used, they can lead to unexpected discoveries. In the language of a dancer, this means that the transformation process crosses sensory boundaries. Thus, the inspiration may appeal to one sense, as in the case of a painting, but ultimately it is transformed into the kinesthetic realm in the form of movement.

Going With the Flow

Once you begin improvising, allow your body to go with the flow of energy that comes forth. Dance is a nonverbal experience, and excessive thinking blocks the body's energy flow. This ability to go with the flow can be compared to the ability to turn off your conscious mind and come to a mental state that is more global and less detailed. Harold Rugg (1963) describes this state as being poised between the **conscious** and **subconscious**—receptive to images and messages from within but in control from without. In other words, you should be sensitive to the inner motivation for movements yet be able to visualize and remember movements as they come forth. Marshall (2002) discusses connecting mind and body in a way in which the body is fully unified, alive, and connected to the mover's inner world while at the same time having a conscious ownership of the actions that come forth. Continued practice in improvisation will help you to identify and summon this receptive state, although it may take many sessions before you're able to readily connect with the condition of mind and body that allows movement to develop freely.

Proper mental imagery is important in many but not all improvisations. For example, you can react to the movements of other dancers rather than be guided by imagery. As you improvise, sensitize yourself to pictures that may appear in your mind. The pictures usually evolve from the inspiration with which you're working. Learn to focus on the images so that you can recall a picture that was particularly interesting or important to you. Jim and Ceci Taylor (1995) suggest that the most vivid and useful images are drawn from your most familiar memories and experiences. Practice moving while you concentrate on your mental images to see what kind of movements come forth.

Developing Your Skills

GOING WITH THE FLOW

As you practice each of the following exercises, try not to think too hard or to anticipate actions as they develop; just let movement happen. It helps to be still at first in order to concentrate on inner movement impulses. Always avoid forcing the process.

Hawkins (1988) recommends closing the eyes to increase concentration when you first begin doing improvisations. For many people, moving with the eyes closed eliminates external distractions and heightens receptivity to internal and personal images. Once you have learned to concentrate, open your eyes and continue to move, but attempt to maintain your **inward focus.**

1. Lie on the floor in a comfortable position. (Use some padding or a mat to help you feel more relaxed.) Take several deep breaths to bring your focus to your body. Begin to allow your body to follow some of the small movements that develop.
2. As a follow-up to the previous exercise, let some of these movements become larger, or let them lead you into new and extended actions.
3. Try the preceding exercises while soft, soothing music is playing.
4. Lie on the floor and visualize a setting in which you feel comfortable and relaxed. Slowly allow your body to begin to move by relating to the qualities or feelings that you experience in this visualized setting.
5. Perform the previous exercise, but gradually begin to change the image or images on which you are focusing. At the same time, allow your movement to change or develop along with the new imagery.

Structuring Improvisational Experiences

Finding and maintaining the right mental state are important for successful improvisation to occur. As discussed earlier, the right mental state is one in which you are concentrating yet relaxed. Sufficient concentration is needed so that mind and body are synchronized and the mind is open to the impulses and flow of movement ideas from the body. Excessive concentration and effort can create tension, blocking the creative pathway between mind and body.

Creating Atmosphere

You can do several things to create conditions that facilitate the kind of mind–body connection desired in an involved improvisation session. First find an environment or place in which you can move comfortably and in which you feel content and tuned in to yourself. Consider size, shape, color, temperature, floor surface, and other factors in selecting an appropriate space for your creative work. Experiment with different spaces before deciding on one. The time of day you choose to work is another important personal consideration in creating the right conditions for improvising. Think about your progression through each day and note when you feel "up"—these "up" times are likely to be your most productive. Try to do your improvising during those periods, because it's difficult to create when you feel dull, bored, or sleepy. When you must work in spaces that are less than ideal, or at times when your energy is low, you'll need to discipline yourself to stay focused. If you're improvising in a dance studio, you may also improve your focus by turning away from the mirrors.

Consider the following points to help you create an atmosphere conducive to creative work. The physical environment—the room in which you choose to improvise—must be large enough to allow freedom of movement and some sense of privacy, particularly if you share the space with other dancers. In addition, you have to allow yourself enough time to get involved in the process of movement discovery. Improvisation also works best in a psychological environment of "openness." Try to maintain an attitude of daring and experimentation without worrying about how your movements will be evaluated. When improvising, use your own judgment and do not think that you need to explain your improvisation to anyone (Schneer 1994). In other words, focus on internal cues, not on external evaluation; remain positive, and have fun during the improvisation process. The ability to get involved in creative activities is largely dependent on having the right feeling. Emotional safety is most important because in such an environment you will feel free to be yourself (Schneer 1994). A final recommendation is to observe others who are more experienced in improvisation to determine how they create an environment that encourages the right frame of mind.

Choosing Appropriate Inspirations

The types of inspirations used during improvisation are also relevant. First, select inspirations for improvisation that suggest movement. Consider that a noun such as *rock* or a verb such as *sit* has little potential to inspire movement. How can you move while trying to create the impression of being a rock? Waves and a river, on the other hand, have a much greater potential to inspire movement. Second, to be more involved, choose inspirations that relate to your world and what you know. Such intrinsic inspirations, coming from your own experiences, will be more interesting and enjoyable. Third, choose inspirations that are structured within a framework of possibilities. The framework allows some openness and gives you the freedom to make choices and work in your own way while limiting your movement choices to a manageable number. For example, improvisations based on body sounds are limited to exploring those sounds; motivations that deal with tactile sensations allow for improvisations within the tactile sphere. Both examples contain a movement-related framework within which you can improvise as opposed to having the entire scope of human movement open to you as a creative possibility.

Finally, consider how different movement inspirations relate to the different **modes of sensing** and **perceiving.** In this book, the inspirations for improvisation are divided into groups, many of which relate to specific **sensory modes.** Movement inspirations, for example, which are kinesthetic, auditory, visual, or even tactile, have already been described. Be sure to practice improvising using inspirations that draw from all those senses. Initially, you may find that some of the inspirations are easier to work with than others. Visually and spatially oriented people, for instance, find visual inspirations more appealing, whereas those who have musical talent may be more creative when using auditory inspirations. The key is to learn to choreograph using inspirations that appeal to a variety of **learning styles** in order to expand your abilities.

Sequencing Experiences

The sequence, or **order,** of inspirations for your improvisational experiences is another concern. According to Hawkins (1988), you should begin a sequence of improvisations with those that are more concrete or structured. Examples are an improvisation dealing with auditory stimuli and one using a prop. Later improvisations should involve feeling reactions to an imaginary situation; those are less concrete and allow you more freedom for individual responses at a time when you should be ready for such responses. It might be worthwhile to repeat feeling-oriented improvisations, because you may need more practice to get involved and relate spontaneously to those inspirations. The most important point is to have a focus or goal while improvising.

Developing Your Skills

IMPROVISATIONS

Examples of improvisations are provided in the following list. Compare these experiences with those suggested for explorations earlier in the chapter, and notice here that the creator has more freedom to supply his or her own ideas. Also, in improvisation you are allowed to continue for a longer time in order to give your own sense of development to the movements. Notice, for example, that the fifth item in Standing Explorations (in Developing Your Skills—Movement Explorations which begins on page 14) began with a specific movement: reaching. Improvisation 3 in the list that follows also begins with a specific movement, or gesture, but is more open ended than the exploration, since you are encouraged to select several gestures from a vast repertoire of human gestures and then vary them. In addition, in the following improvisation, you are encouraged to create a story using these gestures. The exploration, on the other hand, tells you to reach with your arm and to limit variations of the reach to changes in the size of the movement.

As you read each of the following improvisations, pay attention to how the experience progresses. In some improvisations, you are encouraged to explore freely, make some movement selections, and then vary, refine, and develop the selected actions. In other experiences, you begin with a limited number of movement responses that are then developed, varied, and expanded.

1. Improvisations based on auditory stimuli are fun and also provide accompaniment. Move throughout the room trying out different body sounds, such as slapping, clapping, and snapping the fingers. Pick two or three of the body sounds that you like best, and perform those sounds together with appropriate movements. Allow your movements to vary in direction, size, level, and tempo. Vary the order of the sounds and movements, selecting an order that you like. Continue experimenting with the sequence until it fits a specific **pattern** that you can repeat. Practice the sounds and pattern as you move around the dance space, and also notice the patterns that other dancers are performing. See if you can copy the other patterns, then return to your own pattern. Develop one of these patterns into a longer movement sequence.

2. Select an object that has a variety of tactile qualities. Touch this object and explore all its parts. For example, a hand drum is smooth on top of the head, more textured underneath, and angular along the rim; the fasteners that hold the rim to the head are smooth and sometimes cold. Focus on each of the tactile qualities present in the object, and begin to move. (One way to move smoothly is to glide; a possible response to angular shapes is a jagged movement.) Select some of the movements you have discovered and produce your own variations.

3. Pick several of the gestures listed earlier for kinesthetic movement inspirations in the Inspirations and Motivations section on pages 5 to 7, and decide how you can change each gesture. Try changing gesture size, direction, timing, or use of energy. (See the section titled Manipulating Movement in chapter 2 for some suggestions.)

4. Connect the gestures used in the preceding exercise by means of a short story. Integrate each gesture into the story, and then try doing each in the different ways suggested.

5. Props can help you develop many interesting movements. Begin this improvisation by discovering how your prop moves, and then experiment with varying uses of space, time, and energy. Allow your body to travel in different directions and

at different levels as you continue to move your prop. Take note of the ways in which the prop changes or extends the movement of your body (refer to figures 1.3 through 1.5).

6. Imagine that you are in a cool, quiet forest. Observe and respond to this situation. Think about the spongy pine needles beneath your feet, the sunlight filtering through the trees, small animals scampering out of your path, and the closeness of the foliage and vegetation. Begin to move while you focus on how you feel about this imagined situation.

7. You can also create improvisations by using your reactions to a beautiful natural object, such as a seashell. Begin by picking up the shell and examining it carefully. Sense all of its qualities, including its color, **texture,** shape, **line,** and visual patterns. Experience both the visual and the tactile qualities of the shell, exploring and responding to its qualities inside and out. Put the shell down, and move off to your own space in the dance studio. Concentrate on your sensations of and feelings about the seashell. Be quiet initially; focus on your body and your imagery during the transformation process. After you have improvised for a while, find an appropriate conclusion for your movement. An improvisation that develops from feelings and sensory reactions to a shell or other natural object is an example of **abstraction,** which is discussed further in chapter 3.

Solving Improvisational Challenges

A **study** is a short dance, and as such it should have attributes of effective choreography (as described in chapter 3). You'll have many opportunities to do studies in your dance composition classes. The first step in creating a dance study is to discover appropriate movement through improvisation. Here again it is important to know your inspiration or motivation and to concentrate on that motivation when finding movement.

Most of the improvisational inspirations described earlier can be molded into a dance study or a completed dance, although you might use some of the ideas suggested for exploration to develop a dance or study as well. Early studies are usually based on simple **themes,** and as you progress, you will be expected to create studies that are more complex and expressive.

Mental Blocks

As you learn to choreograph you will find that, at times, your work in improvisation flows easily, and at other times, improvising is much more difficult, and you feel "blocked." When that happens, you need to be patient with yourself, since you cannot expect your mind and body always to be equally receptive. Finding ways to work through improvisational problems is part of the process of learning to choreograph (see Developing Your Skills—Solving Improvisational Challenges in the next section).

Remembering New Movements

Many students have trouble remembering movements discovered during an improvisation session, but this problem can be solved through practice. Remembering improvised movement is important because later those movements will be molded and formed into a study or piece of choreography. You will find that the ability to remember movement is comparable to standing outside yourself and watching as you improvise.

Fitting It All Together

You'll also discover that movement ideas do not always come forth in a logical manner. For example, the end of a study or dance may come to you during improvisation before the middle is completed. It requires patience to learn how all the parts fit together; the ability to give form to your choreography takes time. Hawkins (1988) states that each person needs the proper environment and enough practice and encouragement; no two people can be expected to pass through the levels of creative development in the same manner or at the same speed. The goal is for the dance to fit together with a sense of wholeness and to grow from a natural, or **organic,** development of movements and phrases.

Developing Your Skills

SOLVING IMPROVISATIONAL CHALLENGES

1. A dance takes shape in stages, so allow yourself enough time for your creative urges to incubate and emerge.

2. It may help to put your improvisational work aside and come back to it at a later date. Putting your work aside gives your creative ideas time to incubate during the creative process.

3. Open your mind and come up with as many solutions to improvisation problems as possible. Come up with all the movement materials that could be used in your choreography without judging any of them. (It may help to write these movement ideas in a journal.)

4. Next, make a list of all the possible associations that can be attributed to your choreography. Then continue to improvise to see if you can discover new and better movements or phrases.

5. Try breaking your choreographic problem into smaller and more manageable parts, and improvise within a **section** of your dance or within restricted measures of music. When you have found suitable movement, go on to the next section of your choreography.

6. Movement memory can be improved through **repetition.** When you find a movement phrase that feels "right" or about which you have an insight, go back and perform it again. You may need to repeat movements until they fit your imagery or inspiration. As you repeat movements, you should find that those actions begin to be defined and clarified.

7. You can also improve movement memory by improvising while you concentrate on how your movement might look to the audience. This requires making a part of you an external and somewhat uninvolved observer, a skill that comes with practice.

8. One method of fitting the parts of a dance together is to be aware of the evolving shape of your choreography and its development from beginning to end.

9. As you improvise, avoid forcing a composition into a specific form; let form develop naturally in relation to your inspiration. Gradually you should come to know how various movement materials fit together as the dance takes form.

10. If a piece seems to be taking shape in a certain direction, explore that direction even if it differs from your original conception of your work. The creative process requires that you be open to the possibilities as they occur.

Finding the Right Music

Many kinds of music can provide appropriate accompaniment for dance. The goal in selecting music is to find accompaniment that fits the inspiration or intent of your choreography. Doris Humphrey (1987) advised that a dance should not mimic musical structure; the music should be a sympathetic mate, not a master, of the dance. After you gain confidence with the use of accompaniment, you might like to experiment with music that has a feeling different from the inspiration for your dance. You could create a comical effect, for example, by such a mismatch, or you might like to simply use your music as background rather than relating to it in any specific way.

You should consider other criteria when selecting accompaniment. Instrumental music, for instance, usually provides better accompaniment than vocal music because it allows a greater freedom for choreographic interpretation. If you use vocal music, try to avoid movements that pantomime the words; instead, draw from your internal responses. Music with variety in structure, rhythmic patterning, and **quality** also provides better accompaniment, because dancers tend to create repetitious movement when working with music that has little variety.

Try to avoid music performed by large instrumental groups such as a symphony orchestra, since an entire orchestra can overpower the movement of a small number of dancers. Such accompaniment requires a large number of performers to complement its volume and intensity. Small musical groups such as a trio or quartet usually provide excellent accompaniment for dance. Another suggestion is to avoid popular music for your dance compositions. Popular music does not leave freedom for choreographic interpretation because your audience will have heard those pieces many times and might have preconceived ideas about the choreography.

These recommendations refer primarily to accompaniment for **modern dance** and **modern ballet.** In the case of a **classical ballet,** such as *Giselle* or *Coppélia,* accompaniment is determined by historical tradition. Another exception is **jazz** choreography, which is best accompanied by jazz music, although it is preferable to select jazz accompaniment that fits many of the criteria already described. The music used in musical theater productions, on the other hand, is set when a musical is first produced and should not be changed.

Investigate a variety of sources when searching for appropriate accompaniment. Local compact disc stores and libraries can be good sources, particularly if they carry a selection of classical, semiclassical, jazz, and modern or electronic tapes or discs. Look for appropriate music in several sections of these stores or libraries; try checking under the categories of new age, meditation, folk, ethnic, world, historical, contemporary, and jazz music. The music of a flute, harp, or percussion ensemble can also be inspiring. Your radio can be another source of musical ideas; listen carefully, and learn to keep notes on the title, composer, and label of selections that appeal to you. Later you can order the music at a store or from the Internet, or you might find it in a library. Music collections owned by friends can offer some ideas as well. It's even possible to compose your own music or have someone compose it for you. Such accompaniment could be traditional or modern in sound, or it could be developed from words and nonsense syllables.

Working With Copyrights

Once you have selected the accompaniment, be sure to determine whether your music is still under copyright protection. Scores written after 1850 and any recorded music may be protected by copyright (Abeling and Ruskin 1998). Remember to get permission to use copyrighted music in a public performance; you will waste a lot of time if permission is denied after your dance is completed. Your dance teacher should be able to give you some advice concerning regulations governing use of recorded music. In addition, you could talk to professionals who provide legal advice to your group or institution. Some organizations such as Broadcast Music Incorporated and the American Society of Composers, Authors and Publishers can help you with information about copyrighted music, and they may also know if your music has been used by other choreographers (see appendix A for a listing of some of these organizations). Topaz (1995) suggests contacting the music publisher so that a company representative can talk to the composer concerning permission. It is usually customary for choreographers associated with educational institutions to pay a small royalty. Make sure that you receive all permission agreements—including the amount of the royalty—in writing, and keep them on file.

Most composers, particularly those who are young and just getting established, are usually pleased to have you use their music. Many composers are also pleased at the prospect of having a different audience hear their work when it is performed or played at a dance **concert.** Remember to give proper credit in the printed program, and, if possible, invite the composer to the concert. You could also send the composer or the music publisher a video of the completed choreography, but make sure to include all credits on it. Royalty payments are required for the production of musicals and must be negotiated with the owner of those rights.

Working With Your Accompaniment

Before you begin to choreograph, you must know the structure of your music. Listen to your accompaniment carefully and be familiar with its musical **phrasing,** rhythmic patterning, and **tone** (feeling). Katherine Teck (1994) also suggests that you understand the dynamics, pitch, texture, style, and methods of development used in your music. **Dynamics** refers to the degree of loudness, **pitch** to choice of scale and range, **texture** to the density or sparseness of sound, style to the era or cultural context, and development to the materials and methods used to create the score.

If you are using metrically organized music, know how many counts are included in each measure. Most pieces are written in 2/4, 3/4, 4/4, or 6/8 **meter.** Music written in **mixed meter** has a varied number of counts in each bar, or grouping (see figure 1.9). Modern electronic music can have more freedom in terms of metric structure so that you are free to choreograph without counting the music. However, you still have to be aware of the changing sounds and feelings found throughout such accompaniment, because the composer has followed certain patterns in developing the score, and it is the choreographer's job to discover those patterns. The performers must also become familiar with specific sounds in the score and use them as movement cues.

Begin choreographing by listening to your music. Try to maintain a relaxed

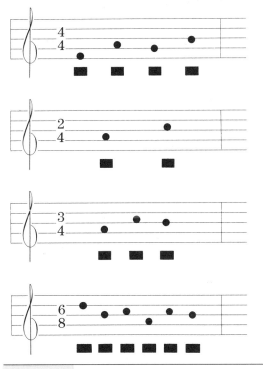

Figure 1.9 It is important for a choreographer to understand how a piece of music is organized. The bold dashes indicate the underlying beats in each measure for different time signatures.

yet concentrated state. You'll discover that the music brings basic ideas or feelings to mind. Continue to concentrate as you begin improvising and transforming your music into movement; you'll see that certain movements and movement phrases come forth. Remember those movements, and if necessary, write them down. Later you can vary and manipulate movements to form the entire composition.

Turn the music off for a while, but continue to concentrate and improvise. This technique should help you clarify your movements. Later return to your accompaniment, performing the movement with the music. You may find yourself repeating this process of concentrating and improvising many times throughout the development of your choreography.

A dance and its accompaniment should fit together. The dance and music should have the following qualities:

- Both should exist in a complementary relationship without one component dominating; each should have a form of its own.
- They should have similar styles and evoke similar feelings in the observer without having the dance mirror or repeat musical structure.
- The choreography and accompaniment should relate and synthesize at certain points throughout the choreography so that the two coexist in a mutually supportive relationship.
- In certain situations, it may be appropriate to use music and movement that are opposite in tone or quality. Such a juxtaposing of sound and action could create tension in a work that is about two people who have opposing viewpoints. The use of music and movement that are opposite in quality could even be comical.

Developing Your Skills

WORKING WITH YOUR ACCOMPANIMENT

1. If you do not understand musical structure, you might want to refer to a basic music text before beginning this set of exercises. Select a metrically organized piece of music, and listen to it to analyze its structure. Write down a description of the structure that includes the underlying pulse (beats), the meter (groupings of beats), and rhythmic patterns that occur in relation to the pulse. Note changes in dynamics, pitch, and texture as well. (Do not use music written in mixed meter.)

2. Clap the underlying pulse in the music you selected in the preceding exercise, then begin to respond to the music by moving with the beat. Allow your body to move on every beat at certain times and over the beat at other times.

3. Listen to the same piece of music to determine how the dynamics, pitch, and texture of the melody change throughout the selection. Improvise movements that fit with these changes. You should find that the music stimulates kinesthetic responses that are high, low, expansive, calm, bold, or frenzied, and so forth, as you hear different musical qualities.

4. Play the same piece of music, and move in a way that produces a simultaneous response to pulse and quality. (Remember that the pulse is the ongoing or underlying beat.)

5. Choose a piece of nonmetric music and improvise with that selection as well. Again notice changes in tone or quality and how those changes affect the quality of your movements.

Exploring Your Movement Inspirations

So now you have read about the creative movement process and had a chance to experience it firsthand in the explorations and improvisations in this chapter. By understanding this process, you should also be better able to cope with problems that may arise during your own dance making. In this chapter you are provided with a diagram, or framework, of the creative process as it can be understood in dance as well. Through this diagram, you learned that creative work begins with observation of your inspiration followed by feeling responses. Those feelings can, in turn, be combined with memories and images in your mind and be transformed into movement materials for your dance. Many possible inspirations are described in this chapter, including various forms of computer technology. Suggestions are offered to help you focus while exploring or improvising by creating an appropriate atmosphere. Information is presented on finding the right music for your dance and how to use your accompaniment in a way that complements your dance.

PRACTICAL APPLICATIONS

CREATE

1. The framework for creating movement presented in this chapter begins with an inspiration. Why is observation of the inspiration important at the beginning of the dance-making process?

2. What are some aspects of an inspiration that can be observed? What, for example, would you observe if your inspiration were a shell or a plant?

3. What are some aspects of the sculptures pictured in figure 1.10, a and b that can be observed in preparation for beginning the dance-making process?

Photos by Robert Eggert. Bronze sculptures by David E. Parvin.

a   b

Figure 1.10   The sculpture in photo (a) is fairly short and static, whereas the sculpture in photo (b) is larger and much more dynamic. Sculpture (a) is titled "Fly Away Home" and sculpture (b) is called "Michelle." In sculpture (a), the figure is blowing a ladybug off her finger, while the dancer in sculpture (b) appears to be moving or falling forward.

4. Your feelings also come into play as part of the framework for creating movement. Briefly describe how you feel about the sculptures in figure 1.10, *a* and *b*.

5. Your memories and imagery are part of the framework for creating movement. How do your memories and experiences contribute to the dance-making process? One way to answer this question is to create a story from a personal memory and tell how that story could contribute to improvisation and dance making. For example, one of my memories is of spending summers on the beaches of Florida paddling in the surf and combing the sand for shells.

6. Do you have any memories or images in mind that could relate to the two pieces of sculpture in figure 1.10, *a* and *b* that would help you create movement? Remember that your imagery can be of many varieties that relate to the various senses.

7. Create two movement sequences that transform your feelings about each of the sculptures in figure 1.10, *a* and *b* into actions. You can also use any relevant memories or images as part of your creative movement process.

PERFORM

1. How can exploration lead to a greater understanding of the motivation for a movement exploration? Give a specific example of a motivation for exploration, perform it, and then explain how performing the exploration led to an increased understanding of the motivation. For example, an exploration of possible movements at the shoulder leads to increased understanding of the movement potential of that joint.

2. How can improvisation lead to a better understanding or appreciation of an inspiration? Give a specific example of an inspiration for an improvisation, and then explain how performing the improvisation led to an increased appreciation of the inspiration.

3. Perform the two movement sequences you created in relation to the pieces of sculpture pictured in figure 1.10, *a* and *b*. Did performing those movements give you any insights about the two pieces of sculpture or change your feelings about them?

4. Perform the two movement sequences you created based on the sculptures again. Which movement sequence was easiest for you to perform? Why do you think that particular sequence was easier for you to perform?

5. Describe how the same two movement sequences felt in your body as you performed them. For example, did they feel expansive, tense, relaxed, flowing?

REFLECT

1. In front of a mirror, perform the same two movement sequences based on the sculptures. How would you describe the two movement sequences? For example, are your movements high or low, and are the shapes you used wide or narrow?

2. Make a video as you perform the two movement sequences. Would your description of the movements change after you saw yourself perform them on the video?

3. Did you find that your movement sequences were similar in any way to either of the sculptures?

4. How were the movements you created different from the two sculptures?

5. Would you make any changes in your movement sequences after viewing them in the mirror or on the video?

Choreography Challenge

Select your favorite inspiration from the list on pages 5 to 7 of this chapter. Then, find an actual example of this inspiration. If your inspiration is a visual pattern, find a picture or photo of a pattern or several patterns. If your inspiration is tactile, find several pieces of cloth or several objects that have an interesting texture when you touch them. Then follow the steps in the next section as they are described in the framework for creating movement.

Prepare for Creating Your Dance

- Once you have selected your inspiration, study it carefully through the process of observation. Notice the details of your inspiration, and decide how it would appeal to the different senses. In fact, you might find that your inspiration appeals to more than one human sense. Ask yourself a series of questions. For example, what colors or patterns do you see when looking at the inspiration? Does the inspiration make a sound or have a particular texture?

- If possible, do some research on your inspiration. Thus, for a painting used as an inspiration, you can research the artist's style and why he or she created the painting. In the case of a pattern on a piece of material, you could research how or where the material was made or what kinds of dyes were used.

- Start to think about elements of the craft that will be a part of the structure of the dance, such as stage spacing, interaction between dancers, and movement variation. Do not focus on those things yet, but be aware of them.

Assess Your Feelings, Memories, and Imagery

- Once you have observed your inspiration and done some research on it, you will need to analyze your feeling response to the inspiration. You may find that you have a single feeling response or that various aspects of the inspiration call forth different feelings.

- Make a list of the different feelings that you have as you observe your inspiration. In addition, decide whether the inspiration calls forth any memories or images, and make a list of them as well.

Explore Insights Through Improvisation

- Begin to move and explore your feeling responses through improvisation.

- At the same time, focus on any images or memories that come to mind as you move. You will probably find that this process takes place in stages over time.

Discover and Transform Movement

- As your improvisation progresses, you will find that you discover various movements. These movements will be the stuff of your dance. Keep track of the movements you discover by writing them in your journal.

- Although it is difficult at this point to know where each movement will fit in your dance, you can begin to think about how you could weave the movements you have discovered into sequences and then into a whole dance.

2

Designing and Shaping the Dance

Choreographers use exploration and improvisation to find movement materials, but it is craft that enables them to shape these movement materials into a dance—a process of finding possibilities and then putting the pieces of the puzzle together. This chapter relates to the fourth Dance Standard, which addresses how to apply creative and critical-thinking skills to dance making (National Dance Association 1996). You'll learn how to manipulate space, time, energy, and shape by experimenting with the many suggestions provided for ways in which movement can be varied using these **elements.** For example, say that one of the movements you discover during improvisation is to turn and then drop to the floor. Through movement manipulation, however, you can create many variations of these movements, such as turning slowly and dropping quickly to the floor or turning quickly and descending slowly to the floor. You will need to use your critical-thinking skills to decide which of the movement variations you have created fits what you are trying to say or do in your dance. Choreography has the power to communicate, or have an impact, but the success of the communication, or impact, depends on the final form of the work. You will also learn to use stage space, **unison, sequence, opposition,** and groups of dancers in relation to the intent of your dance. An analysis of some of the techniques discovered by the postmodern dancers follows. You're encouraged to explore these techniques to make dances as well. The chapter ends with a description of various forms of technology that have been used to extend the creativity of the choreographer.

Once you have found movement and movement phrases through improvisation, you can begin to mold your dance. This is the point at which the craft of choreography becomes important. Choreographic craft is the ability of the choreographer to give form to movement so that the dance has a sense of wholeness. A knowledge of craft also involves the process of movement manipulation—the varying and extending of movement. Through manipulation, movements remain compelling in repetition because their appearance has been changed and varied. By using craft, the choreographer knows where to place the dancers in the stage space to achieve maximum effect. With appropriate placement of dancers on the stage, you can heighten projection of movement and create meaningful relationships between performers.

The materials presented in chapters 2 and 3 take you into the fourth stage of the creative process—sessions in evaluation. Through the tools of craft, you as the choreographer can check out the possibilities and see what works by using aesthetic judgment. You can determine the final form and organization of a dance by experimenting with various solutions. In terms of the framework for creating movements and dances, you will work with movements you have already discovered by varying them and by arranging and rearranging those movements (see figures 1.1 and 1.2). As stated in chapter 1, the dance-making process is circular in nature, so you can interrupt varying the movement by returning to your inspiration to discover new movements. You may even put your work on a dance aside for a while and return to it later.

Manipulating Movement

You may have discovered that in the foregoing explorations that it was easier for you to perform certain aspects of the elements in a specific way. For example, you might prefer a large use of space, fast movements, sustained energy, or rounded body shapes. Movements that are easier to perform, or that feel more comfortable, probably fit with your innate movement preferences. Keep in mind, however, that you should try to expand your use of space, time, energy, and body shape in order to increase your movement vocabulary. A varied use of these elements, through a process called **movement manipulation,** will also enable you to create dances that are more varied and stimulating for the audience.

I have often used movement manipulation as a teaching tool in choreography classes. Manipulating "known" movement allows creativity to take place within a solid framework so that the creative "unknown" is digested in very small bites. One of my former students, whose dance experience consisted of ballet technique and performance, was able to begin experimenting with movement using the manipulation approach. By the end of the term, she had gained enough confidence to create a dance using **percussive** movement. She had taken a big step, since her final choreography was considerably different from the style of the dance form she had studied up to that point. Manipulation, a rather concrete process, allowed that student to experiment with movement and extend her vocabulary beyond her comfort zone of soft, graceful movement.

Through manipulation, the choreographer varies movements based on an understanding of the elements space, time, energy, and shape. Each of these, in turn, is an important aspect of all human actions. Movement occurs in space, takes time, is propelled by energy, and goes through a series of specific body shapes as the performers execute it.

Choreographers use manipulation to create movement **variety** in any dance form. You can change the use of space, time, energy, or body shape of any action or have dancers perform the same actions on different pathways with a different use of focus or arm movements. Such variations are fun to learn and frequently test coordination at the same time.

Space

The movement element space refers to the area occupied by dancers and to how dancers move in and around the area. The concept also includes how the choreographer chooses to mold and design aspects of space. Space can be divided into aspects of direction, size, level, and focus.

A movement can go forward, to either side, and backward. Human movement can also travel in a variety of diagonal directions, including the two diagonals in front and the two diagonals in back of the body (see figure 2.1). Dancers can move the body in all eight directions or may simply **face** the body in any of the eight directions. (The concept of eight basic directions is used here as a point of orientation, although in reality the dancer can also move or face directions that fall between the eight.) In addition, dancers can trace many different pathways, or floor patterns, by moving and continually changing direction.

Choreographers can play with the possibilities in size by making an action larger or smaller. They can also change the level—high, medium, or low—and alter a dancer's use of focus, since dancers can focus in many different

Figure 2.1   Facing dancers in different directions creates a varied effect for the audience. The dancer facing the back lacks the feeling and expression projected by the other three dancers.

directions while still performing the same movement series (see figure 2.2, *a* through *c*). All of these changes make the same movement look different and allow the choreographer to use movements more than once in a dance. You can learn to vary the spatial element through the skill-development exercises provided.

a

b

c

Figure 2.2   *(a)* The three dancers demonstrate a gradually widening, or larger, movement from right to left. *(b)* The three basic levels of movement are high, middle, and low. *(c)* Changing focus from normal or middle level to high level alters the appearance of a body shape or movement.

Developing Your Skills

SPACE

Direction

The following explorations deal with direction, an aspect of space.

1. Stand in one spot and perform a simple axial movement, such as bending, twisting, reaching, or stretching. Observe yourself in a mirror while you do this movement, and then try doing the same movement while you face your body in different directions.

2. Walk across the space using a variety of directions, such as forward, backward, sideways, or any of the four diagonals.

3. Use a basic walk to move around the space. As you walk, begin to change direction on specific counts. Practice changing direction on every eighth, fourth, and second count. Then see what it feels like to change direction on every count.

4. Walk for 16 counts, but change direction on specific counts of your own choosing. Try several variations of this exploration by altering the direction of your walk on different counts.

5. Perform steps 2 to 4 using other locomotor actions, such as run, hop, jump, slide, skip, leap, or gallop.

6. Design a movement sequence of 24 counts in length. Use three different axial movements and two different locomotor movements to create the pattern. Create a variation of this 24-count sequence by changing the direction of some of the movements.

7. Watch a video of a dance created by a well-known choreographer. Then select a short movement sequence from that dance, and experiment with the sequence by performing it in different directions. If possible, have another dancer perform the movement sequence using the directional changes. Does the sequence look different to you when it is performed in the new directions?

Size

The following explorations deal with the spatial aspect of size.

1. Select a common human gesture, such as waving. Experiment with the gesture to see how small it can become.

2. Perform the previous gesture repeatedly, but allow it to become increasingly larger until it can become no larger. Notice the difference in the kinesthetic feeling when the movement is performed large, smaller, or in a medium size.

3. Try varying the size of a locomotor movement, such as walking. Again, notice how it feels to vary the size of the movement. You may also notice that there is a normal, or comfortable, size in which to perform most actions.

4. Create a 30-count sequence by using several typical human gestures combined with locomotor movement. You could base the development of the pattern on a story. Then change the sequence by changing the size of some of the movements. Decide how those changes affect the appearance of the pattern.

Level

The following explorations deal with the spatial aspect of level.

1. Walk around the space while changing the level of your walking from middle to high to low. Be sensitive to the different body feelings associated with the level changes.

2. Try altering the level of some of the other locomotor movements.

3. Walk and change level every eighth, fourth, and second count. Then try changing level on every count as you walk.

4. On separate sheets of paper, list 10 common actions, such as pushing, sitting down, or picking up an object. Select five of the sheets and combine the movements listed into a sequence. Then decide how many times you will perform each movement and the order in which you will perform the actions. (You might need to provide **transitional** movements between the actions.) Finally, create a variation of your sequence by making several changes in the level at which you perform the movements.

5. Return to the movement sequence you worked with in step 7 in the section titled Developing Your Skills—Direction. Then, make some changes in the size and level of those movements as well.

Focus and Floor Pattern

The following explorations deal with the spatial aspects of focus and floor pattern.

1. Walk around your dance space, and change your focus (the direction of your face and eyes as you walk). Notice the different feeling that accompanies walking while looking down, up, and to the side.

2. As you walk, focus first in the direction of your movement and then away from your movement direction. Repeat this altered use of focus several times.

3. Using walking steps, trace a simple geometric pattern, such as a circle, square, or triangle, on the floor. This geometric shape is your floor pattern.

4. As a continuation to exploration 3, alter the direction of your focus as you continue to walk in the same geometric floor pattern.

5. Choreograph the changes of focus in the preceding step by performing them at set intervals, but continue to move through the same floor pattern.

6. Draw a new floor pattern on a piece of paper. The pattern should carry you across and around the entire dance space. See if you can use both curved and straight pathways in the floor pattern. Move through your pattern using walking steps to trace it on the floor. You should notice that, as you move through the pattern, changes in direction are already taking place. Trace your pathway again on the floor, and this time try changing your focus. You can create other variations by adding **silences** and by changing the size or level of some of the movements.

7. You can create another interesting spatial variation by adding arm movements to the floor pattern you created. You will discover that the arms can trace many different pathways in space while the feet and legs continue to follow the same pathway on the floor using the same locomotor steps. Try moving the arms in a circular pathway and then in a sharp (angular) pathway.

8. Altering the use of the body is another way to add variety to your movements. Change the position of the body while tracing the same floor pattern as in the preceding exploration. Try curving the body forward from the waist, arching the

upper back, or even tilting the torso to the side as you move through the pattern (see figure 2.3).

9. Perform this pattern or combination of movements backward, starting at the end and progressing to the beginning.

10. You can make floor patterns by tracing your name on the floor or by using randomly selected letters and numbers placed in a sequence.

Figure 2.3   Different ways of placing the arms and body also change the way movement looks.

Timing

Choreographers often play with variations in **timing.** You'll find that manipulation of tempo (speed) of your movements is easier if you move with an underlying sound, known as the beat or pulse. Once the beat is established, you can try changing timing by moving faster or more slowly than the beat. Understanding how to use the element of time involves working with changes in **accent** and **rhythm** as well. You can create accents by making a movement stronger or larger to produce a point of emphasis in a sequence. Rhythms or rhythmic patterns are generated when a dancer moves at a varying tempo in a movement sequence or within a specific number of beats (see figure 2.4). Adding silences, or places where you hold a pose or body shape, also contributes to rhythmic patterning.

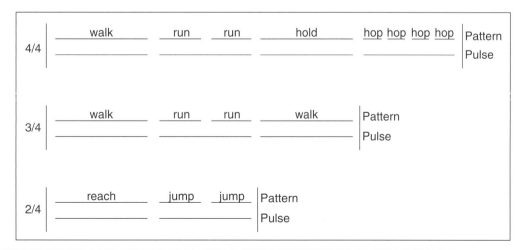

Figure 2.4   The upper row of dashes indicates a rhythmic pattern over the underlying beat shown in the lower row of dashes.

From Modern Dance, Body and Mind, A Basic Approach for Beginners 2nd edition by MINTON. 1991. Adapted with permission of Brooks/Cole, a division of Thomson Learning: www.thomsonrights.com. Fax 800-730-2215.

Developing Your Skills

TIMING

1. Pick a simple movement, such as an arm circle. Gradually increase the tempo of the action, and then slow it down.

2. Try increasing and decreasing the tempo of a locomotor step. You will find that some movements can be done faster, but others cannot be performed skillfully at a more rapid speed. Actions in elevation, for example, can't be slowed to any great degree. Try to take this exercise as far as you can by experimenting with extreme changes of tempo.

3. Choose one of the floor patterns you developed while experimenting with the use of space, and make some changes in the timing of some of the movements. Try to vary the tempo of the pattern at several points. Compare the variations.

4. Insert some silences into one of the floor patterns you developed in the section titled Focus and Floor Pattern.

5. You can also vary timing by introducing points of emphasis, known as accents. Walk around the dance space and perform a movement with one arm to indicate points of accent in your walk. Try performing the accents on specific beats. For example, in 4/4 meter, accent counts 1 and 3; then try putting the emphasis on counts 2 and 4. Putting the accents on counts 2 and 4 creates a pulling feeling known as **syncopation.** Experiment with the use of accents in 2/4, 3/4, and 6/8 meters as well.

6. Do the previous exploration using other parts of your body to produce the movement accents.

7. Move around the dance space while taking one step on each beat of your music. Then create rhythms by altering the tempo of your movement. In other words, you will move faster, slower, or on the musical pulse at various times.

8. Create a single rhythmic pattern that is eight counts long. This exploration might be easier to understand if you make a diagram of the rhythmic pattern first (refer again to figure 2.4). First, try clapping the pattern, and finally create the same pattern with movement. See if you can perform the pattern more than once without altering it.

9. Create a longer rhythmic pattern that includes some silences.

10. Create a third rhythmic pattern, and practice the pattern using sound. Teck (1994) suggests using body sounds such as slaps, swipes, rubbing, scratching, thumping the fist on the chest, and finger snapping to provide a range of dynamics and pitch. Try to repeat the pattern with movement alone.

11. Turn your television on and select a program in which the performers are gesturing with their hands and upper body. Turn off the sound and begin to copy some of the gestures you see on the screen. Then, perform those gestures at a different speed, making them faster or slower than the original performance. Did the gestures feel different in your body when you performed them at a different speed?

You will find new movement patterns taking shape as you experiment with changes of tempo and with the addition of accents and silences. Compare the rhythm of the new patterns with those in the original.

Dance Energies

Energy, or **force,** propels movement. Force initiates movement, but sometimes it is also needed to stop action. Energy in dance can be channeled in six basic ways, known as qualities: sustained, percussive, vibratory, swinging, suspended, and collapsing.

- In **sustained** movement, the dancer moves smoothly, continuously, and with flow and control. Sustained movement can be stopped easily at any point during the action. It lacks accents and an obvious beginning and ending.

- In contrast to sustained movement, percussive movements are explosive or sharp. They are accented with jabs of energy and have an obvious start and stop. Small percussive actions can be described using the word *staccato.*

- **Vibratory** movement, as the term suggests, consists of trembling or shaking. It produces a jittery effect that is really a much faster version of percussive actions.

- **Swinging** movement traces an arc, or curved line, in space. When you perform swinging movement, allow your body to relax and give in to gravity on the downward part of the motion, followed by an upward application of energy. The length of the swinging body part and the nature of the joint determine the speed and rhythm of the swing. A swing is also very repetitive.

- Dancers performing **suspended** actions hover in space, creating the illusion of defying gravity. The high point of a leap has a feeling of suspension, as does the end of an inhalation of breath that accompanies movement.

- The sixth energy quality is a release of tension, or **collapsing.** A collapse can be performed at a slow or fast tempo. A dancer using a slow collapse gradually gives in to gravity, making a slow, controlled descent to the floor. A slow collapse could be described as a melting or oozing action in a downward direction, whereas with a fast collapse, the dancer drops suddenly to the floor with less control.

A varied use of energy eliminates the monotony of performing all movements with the same quality. Choreographers should also use the six qualities to complement changes in the tone of the accompaniment or in relation to the meanings to be communicated in the dance.

Developing Your Skills

DANCE ENERGIES

1. Kinesthetic understanding of energy quality can be enhanced through vocalization. In this exercise, you will sing and perform the various energy qualities. For example, a continuous blowing or whistling sound could be used with sustained movement; a harsh shout or a grunt could be used with percussive actions; and sounds made with vibratory movement could be intermittent, such as the sound made by flapping the tongue rapidly across the upper lip. After you discover sounds to fit each of the six energy qualities, try moving and making sounds at the same time to provide a kind of self-accompaniment. You should perform the movements in the same quality as the accompanying vocal sounds.

2. Select a single movement such as pushing, and perform the action using each of the six qualities. Focus on the different kinesthetic feeling each energy quality produces in your body, and notice how changes in quality produce changes in the use of space and time as well.

3. Think of a long word with multiple syllables. Decide how many times you wish to say each syllable and then say the separate syllables with a different vocal quality. Create movements to complement each of the vocal qualities you used throughout the word.

4. Choose a series of movements or movement phrases you learned in dance technique class. Practice the pattern, and then change the energy quality in several places. Experiment with various uses of energy throughout the movement combination.

5. Create your own movement combination by linking a series of axial and loco-motor actions together. Determine the number and order of the axial and loco-motor movements in your pattern, and then practice that pattern several times. Finally, vary the movement combination by making several changes in your use of energy.

6. Use the same gestures from the television program in this exploration that you used in exercise 11 from the timing section, but this time change the quality of the actions. Did changing the movement quality of the gestures alter their appearance?

Individual Body Shapes

Shape, as used in this section, refers to the configuration of body parts, or how the entire body is molded in space. The body can be rounded, angular, or a combination of the two. Dancers can take on and discover many shapes as they move, and choreographers can use changing body shapes to vary movement. Other body shapes can vary from wide to narrow and from high to low. It is also possible to create balanced, or **symmetrical,** shapes and unbalanced, or **asymmetrical,** shapes with your body. In a symmetrical body shape, the right and left sides of the body match. This means that if the dancer were a flat piece of paper, the paper could be folded down the middle and the two sides would be identical. With asymmetrical body shapes the two sides of the body do not match. Asymmetrical shapes are more exciting to watch because they are off center and look unstable as if the dancer is getting ready to move (see figure 2.5).

Figure 2.5   The downstage dancer is in an asymmetrical body shape, whereas the upstage dancer is positioned symmetrically.

Developing Your Skills

INDIVIDUAL BODY SHAPES

1. Let your body assume a shape, and concentrate on the kinesthetic feeling of that shape. For instance, you might explore the different kinesthetic feelings of expansive and then narrow shapes. Try another body shape, and be aware of the kinesthetic feeling or feelings that accompany it.

2. Use a full-length mirror to study the various shapes you can make with your body. Experiment with many variations, such as high, low, wide, narrow, rounded, and angular.

3. Find several symmetrical shapes and several asymmetrical shapes with your own body. Look at each of the body shapes in the mirror and decide why each type looks different to you. Which type of body shape looks more exciting?

4. Practice moving around the dance space, stopping suddenly in an interesting shape. (You can use a cue to stop your actions, such as someone clapping or beating a drum. Then assume a shape when the sound stops.)

5. Put some of the shapes you have discovered into a series. Practice moving from one shape to another. Vary the way in which you move between the body shapes by altering how you use space, time, or energy during the transitions. For example, you could move very slowly or very fast between body shapes; you might change shape by using a straight pathway or a curved pathway; or you could change the quality of energy used to make transitional movements.

6. Choose a prop and begin to move. Be aware of the many shapes that can be created with the prop. Use a mirror to observe how shapes made with the prop can be combined with those made by your body.

7. Assume a body shape, and relate that shape to the shape made by another dancer. Move with the other dancer, allowing the shapes formed by both of your bodies to intertwine in space. Move over, under, around, and through the shapes made by your partner. Be aware of how you both move from shape to shape. Try to remember the sequence of shapes and transitions that you created so that you and your partner are able to do them again. Create some variations of this sequence by changing aspects of space, time, and energy as indicated in the preceding sections (see figure 2.6).

Figure 2.6   The dancers are moving and relating one body shape to another.

8. Study the computer-generated visual design presented in figure 2.7. Then, select several of the shapes in that design and use your body or a part of your body to copy the shapes.

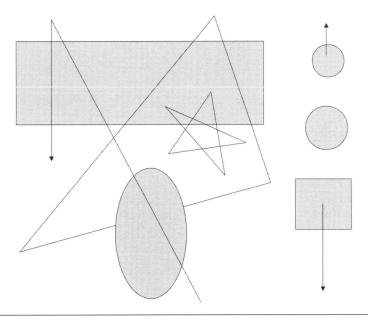

Figure 2.7   Computer-generated design using PowerPoint.

Group Shapes

Dancers can move through many different group shapes as they perform a piece of choreography. The choreographer creates the shapes by designing groupings of dancers and by arranging the groups in ways that are wide, narrow, rounded, angular, symmetrical, or asymmetrical.

When working with group shapes, the dancers should be viewed together as a total picture or arrangement within a picture frame. A symmetrical grouping is one in which the shapes made by the dancers on one side of the group mirror the shapes on the other side of the arrangement. In an asymmetrical grouping, the use of body shapes is unbalanced, and one side of the arrangement does not match the other (see figure 2.8, a and b). When arranging such groupings, see the total visual picture created by the dancers, and notice the **focal point** of the visual design. It is also necessary for choreographers to see such groupings as dynamic rather than static. The essence of dance is motion, not a stagnant positioning of performers. If dancers do hold a grouping, make the grouping interesting and have the dancers retain a sense of energy so that the group shape remains alive.

a

b

Figure 2.8   *(a)* A symmetrical grouping of three dancers; *(b)* an asymmetrical grouping.

Developing Your Skills

GROUP SHAPES

1. Practice grouping dancers by forming several symmetrical groupings. Then position dancers in several groupings that are asymmetrical. If performers are well placed, your eye travels comfortably around the whole arrangement. See if you can find the focal point for each grouping, and look at the kind of lines that the performers create in space with their arms and legs. Try groupings in which all of the dancers make straight lines with the parts of their bodies. Experiment with groupings in which all body lines are curved. Finally, mix straight and curved body lines in the same grouping.

2. Try adding movement to your groupings by having the dancers move around the space while retaining a group shape. Then have them move throughout a grouping rather than stopping and holding the shape. Have your dancers make transitional movements from one grouping to another. The transitions can consist of **direct pathways,** which take the dancers directly from one grouping to another, or they can be longer, and more roundabout, **indirect pathways.**

3. Try building a group shape. Begin by having one dancer assume a shape, then have the other dancers connect to the first dancer to gradually form the whole group. You can continue to build new arrangements by moving the first dancer to a new location to begin a new group shape. (This exploration is easier if all dancers are given a number to indicate when they move to a new location.)

Negative space is another aspect of both individual and group shapes. The term refers to the spaces between parts of a dancer's body as well as to the spaces between individual dancers (see figure 2.9).

Figure 2.9 The spaces between parts of the dancers' bodies and between the dancers are negative spaces. A focal point of the whole design is located at the waistline of the middle dancer.

Developing Your Skills

NEGATIVE SPACE

1. Look again at some of the shapes you can make with your own body. As you look at those shapes in the mirror, notice how the spaces between parts of your body are also part of the overall shape.

2. Practice moving in various shapes, and watch the changes in the sizes and shapes of the negative spaces.

3. Arrange several dancers in a group shape, and notice the sizes and shapes of the negative spaces.

4. Following on exploration 3, have the dancers move in the group shape, and again focus on the changes in the negative spaces.

5. Choreograph a series of group shapes that emphasize the spaces between the dancers and the spaces between the parts of their bodies.

Arranging Movement for Effective Communication

Communication through movement is sometimes the aim in choreography. At other times, choreographers design compositions emphasizing movement alone. In the latter type of dance, one of the goals is to experiment with variations by manipulating movements in terms of space, time, energy, and shape.

In either case, the movements have a message for audience members, because the potential for **nonverbal communication** is difficult to avoid. From the early years, children learn to recognize certain gestures, and each gesture has a message based on life experiences. Waving, for instance, is a friendly gesture, whereas a slapping or striking action is interpreted as aggressive or threatening. Humphrey (1987) said that no movement would be made at all without its being initiated by some type of motivation.

Hawkins (1988) believes that movements transmit feelings because of the way in which the elements are used in the movements. Although essentially all people have learned to recognize the varied use of the elements, the recognition usually is subconscious. An expansive use of space, for example, is usually recognized as being bold; a small use of space could be timid or tentative. Likewise, viewers can see upward focus as uplifting and downward focus as sad. Dancers who perform quick, darting movements can portray urgency or perhaps anger, and those who move slowly usually appear tired or calm. A low energy level suggests weakness, while many find energetic movement to be strong.

Developing Your Skills

EFFECTIVE COMMUNICATION

1. When out in public, learn to observe the movements of others—it can be a fascinating experience. Be aware of the way in which people carry their bodies and how their posture is organized. Many people have a postural orientation that causes a forward tilt as they walk. Others lean backward as they move, or they poke their chins out in front of their bodies (see figure 2.10). Also watch the gestures people use while talking to each other. Relate your observations to the use of space, time, energy, and shape involved. Keep a notebook or journal of the various actions

Figure 2.10 Various uses of posture project various feelings to the viewer.

you see (see figure 2.11). As you observe, keep in mind that many human gestures are specific to a culture.

2. Return to the television program you were watching in order to do the exercises in the section titled Developing Your Skills—Timing. Keep the volume turned down, and read the message or messages that are communicated through the use of gesture you see on the screen.

3. If there is more than one person on the screen, compare the message communicated through the gestures used by each person. Do the two sets of gestures match, or are they different in terms of the message sent?

Figure 2.11 We have learned to interpret the meaning of gestures such as reaching, waving, and punching. Such interpretations are based on how space, time, energy, and shape are used in the gestures.

4. Return to the dance created by the well-known choreographer that you viewed in the section titled Developing Your Skills—Direction. This time, however, look at the dancers' performance by studying their use of space, time, energy, and body shape. What message is communicated through the use of those elements?

Creating a Total Picture

As you view your choreography, imagine it as a painting or series of paintings enclosed in a frame. Onstage, the picture frame is already in place in the shape of the **proscenium** arch that surrounds the stage; your dancers are the colors, lines, and shapes in your painting (see figure 2.12). Decide whether everything fits together to make up a total picture. Be aware of the space between and around your dancers, since that space is also part of the total vision you create. You may notice that the space between dancers will appear to be moving as if it had a life of its own. This is true because this space becomes part of the dance as well.

Many dance critics have tried to analyze why the empty space onstage becomes part of the choreography. Before a dance is performed, the audience sees an empty stage as an expanse of open space. Hawkins (1988) says that it is the choreographer's job to design movement that brings the space to life, because an empty stage is dead until a dancer moves through and around the space. Many think that the energized nature of the space is an illusion created by

Figure 2.12 The proscenium arch surrounds the stage like a picture frame.

the performers' ability to throw energy outward. Langer (1957), a philosopher, has described the illusion created in a dance as a **virtual entity**—one that is different from the actual physical components of bodies in motion. The virtual entity of the dance is real because we see it, but it lacks the concrete nature of our physical world. In other words, the choreographer creates a magical entity for the audience—an entity that consists of many separate movements, shapes, and energies but that, in a successful dance, forms a whole from beginning to end. The more successful the choreography, the less the actual physical components of a dance will be noticed. It is essential to think of your choreography in terms of a whole and to keep this entity in mind when working on any part of the entire dance.

Developing Your Skills

CREATING A TOTAL PICTURE

1. Watch a dancer move straight across the space in front of you. (You should notice how the corridor of space becomes energized, or alive.)

2. Continuing from exercise 1, watch while the same dancer moves throughout the entire space. (You should notice a growing visual awareness of the whole studio.)

3. Have the same person stand in one spot and move his or her arms and legs in different directions. (You should see the sphere, or area surrounding the dancer's body, come alive.)

4. Repeat exploration 3 with more than one dancer, and then compare that effect to the one created previously.

5. Experiment with the location of each dancer in exercise 4. Does the change in location affect your awareness of the entire space?

Staging the Dance

A choreographer usually stages a dance following the work in movement discovery and manipulation already described. Staging a composition involves several steps, the first of which is to decide on an order for the selected actions. Then the choreographer determines which actions each dancer is to perform and how the dancers are placed and moved around the stage space. During this process, the choreographer may move each dancer singly or arrange them in interesting groupings to create well-proportioned pictures. Beginning choreographers should consider the following ideas to help stage their choreography.

- Dancers can move in many directions, including toward the audience, or **downstage,** and away from the audience, or **upstage.** Movement to the side is to **stage right** or **stage left,** according to the performer's orientation.

- The stage is also divided into a number of **areas** that differ in relative importance so that movements performed in each of the stage areas can have a varying impact. According to Humphrey (1987), dancers positioned at center stage attract the most attention, and a solo or lead dancer should perform at center stage. On the other hand, the center should not be emphasized continuously, because its power is easily weakened through overuse. Upstage dancers appear remote or mysterious, whereas downstage action is more intimate and is often reserved for comedy. The areas at the side, to stage right or left, are weak (see figure 2.13).

- Various pathways onstage differ in terms of importance. Dancers who execute movement in straight paths appear strong and direct. It is very powerful, for example, to advance from an upstage position directly downstage toward the audience, because the dancer becomes visually larger while traveling on this path (see figure 2.14).

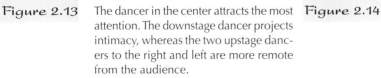

Figure 2.13 The dancer in the center attracts the most attention. The downstage dancer projects intimacy, whereas the two upstage dancers to the right and left are more remote from the audience.

Figure 2.14 The dancer closest to the audience has moved downstage and appears larger and more powerful.

Movement done on the diagonal pathway from an upstage to a downstage corner is powerful as well. Curved pathways lack the strength of movement performed in straight paths; when a performer follows a curved pathway, the body facing changes constantly, and the visual impression is less forceful.

- Choreographers block, or arrange the movement sequences, in a dance by being aware of how the dancers move in relation to each other. When you work with groups of several dancers, do not place the downstage performers directly in front of those who are upstage. An overlapping arrangement of dancers can be very effective, but there is no reason to place a performer upstage if the downstage performer completely blocks that dancer (see figures 2.15, *a* through *c*). On the other hand, choreographers should not position dancers in extreme stage-right or stage-left positions when those dancers are part of one group. The extreme placement of performers divides the audience's attention, making it impossible to focus on either dancer for any length of time

a

b

c

Figure 2.15 *(a)* An example of poor blocking; *(b)* improved appearance of a group of dancers through better spacing; *(c)* an interesting effect can be achieved by placing one dancer directly in front of another dancer, if this fits the intent.

(see figure 2.16). However, do use a divided focus if there is a reason for having each dancer or group of dancers viewed separately.

- The direction in which dancers face is equally important. Choreographers should instruct dancers to face in a way that allows action to be viewed to the greatest advantage, not in a direction in which part of the movement is hidden. Arm or leg movements executed in front of the body, for example, cannot be seen when the dancer is facing upstage. Similarly, the audience cannot see an **arabesque** when it's performed with the body facing directly toward the audience; a diagonal or side facing should be used for an arabesque instead. In addition, diagonal facings are often a much more pleasing way to view a dancer's body (see figure 2.17, *a* and *b*). Take care and use discretion when placing dancers in ways that could be offensive to the audience. For example, positions that expose female breasts or the crotch could be objectionable to some people.

Figure 2.16 The audience sees these two dancers separately rather than as part of one group.

a   *b*

Figure 2.17 *(a)* An example of poor use of facing, hiding the overall shape of the movement; *(b)* improved facing.

- The performer's **facial expression** may have bearing on the intent of choreography. Choreographers should consider the dancers' faces when positioning them in the stage space, since facial expressions can enhance the appeal of a work. Remember that the impassive face is most appropriate for choreography that is devoid of feelings or messages.

Occasionally, there is a need to choreograph a **dance in the round.** A dance choreographed in the round is designed so it can be viewed from more than one direction. This choreographic approach contrasts with dances designed for a proscenium, or picture frame, stage in which the piece is viewed only from the front. Dance in the round presents numerous possibilities, but the choreographer's job is more complex because the performers are viewed from all directions. When choreographing in the round, consider **blocking,** facing, and direction from all perspectives.

Developing Your Skills

STAGING THE DANCE

1. Have a group of dancers stand in various positions in the studio, and notice where your eye is drawn. The dancer at center should attract the most attention. Assess the relative impact of the dancers who are standing in other areas of the studio. Experiment by placing the center or solo dancer at different points in the space. You may decide that you prefer to position that dancer somewhere else.

2. Watch a single dancer use straight and then curved pathways to move around the space. Decide whether straight or curved paths have a more powerful effect.

3. Watch while one dancer walks slowly and in a straight line from upstage center to downstage center. Notice how much larger and more powerful the dancer appears in the downstage position. Watch the same dancer walk slowly from an upstage to a downstage corner.

4. Arrange three dancers at points that are far apart in the studio space. Gradually move those three dancers closer together and decide at what point the dancers can be viewed as one group rather than as separate dancers.

5. Following from exercise 4, group the three dancers so that their bodies overlap. Arrange and rearrange them so that their bodies overlap to a greater or lesser degree. Decide which effect you like the best. Finally, try grouping the dancers so that the bodies of the upstage dancers are hidden, and then have all the dancers move their arms and legs.

6. Select a body shape, and have a dancer assume that shape. Ask the dancer to face in different directions, and then decide which facing is most complementary. Notice how some of the facings hide parts of the dancer's body.

7. Have a dancer repeat a movement sequence using different facial expressions. Decide what effect, if any, the changed expressions have on movement projection or communication.

Arranging Dancers in Space and Time

There are many ways in which your dancers can be arranged in space and time throughout a piece. Unison, sequence, and opposition provide three possible ways in which you can arrange movement. It could also be effective to try other possibilities or to have all your dancers do entirely different movements at any point in your choreography.

Dancers relate in both space and time throughout a single piece of choreography. Unison movement, or having all the dancers do the same movement simultaneously, is one way choreographers can arrange dancers with respect to timing. While unison movement can be strong and powerful, it is boring when used repeatedly in a composition, and it is weak when not performed with precision by all the dancers in a group.

Another technique choreographers use to set timing in a piece is to have the dancers begin the same movement sequence on different counts. Dancer 1, for example, begins moving on count 1 of a sequence; dancers 2 and 3 in the **ensemble** start on counts 2 and 3, respectively. Hayes (1955) calls such an arrangement **sequential** movement, because it creates an overlapping effect; movements are seen once and are then seen again a little later. Choreographers can create sequential movement by having dancers enter the stage at different times or by stopping the action and having the performers begin again on different counts (see figure 2.18).

A third method for arranging movement, called opposition, involves an understanding of both space and time. Opposition, which means

Figure 2.18 An example of sequential movement design.

that the dancers move in opposite directions in space, can be developed from unison or sequential actions. In opposition, the performers move from side to side or travel diagonally between upstage and downstage corners. Opposition creates an effect in which the negative space between and surrounding the dancers seems to narrow and widen as they move toward or away from one another (see figure 2.19, a and b). Dancers can also achieve the effect of opposition by rotating their bodies in opposite directions.

a

b

Figure 2.19 Use of opposition. Notice (a) the space between the dancers as well as the area surrounding them, and (b) opposition on a diagonal and more vertical direction.

Developing Your Skills

UNISON, SEQUENCE, OPPOSITION

1. Develop a short movement sequence, and teach the sequence to a small group of dancers. Have all the dancers perform the sequence by beginning their movement on the same count. You'll notice that the dancers must perform unison movement in the same way, since differences in execution are noticeable.

2. Select a single action, such as reaching upward. To produce a sequence of actions, have each dancer begin one or two counts later than the dancer to the right or left. Sequential actions usually produce a wave or domino effect.

3. You can create vertical opposition by having two dancers stand close together; while one dancer moves up, the other one goes down. You can create side-to-side opposition using a swaying action, and you can create turning opposition by having the dancers turn in opposite directions. Notice how opposition produces a pulling feeling and how the negative spaces between the dancers expand and contract.

4. Teach three entirely different movement phrases to three dancers. Have the three dancers simultaneously perform their own sequence, and then experiment with the location of each dancer with the goal of achieving a unified effect.

Choreographic Ideas From Postmodern Dance

Many professional dancers have experimented with new choreographic forms and ideas in the past 50 years. Some innovative, or **experimental,** dance forms still exist, and others have vanished. In either case, novice choreographers can profit by studying the structure, development, and content used by innovative artists, sometimes known as **postmodern** dancers, or postmoderns.

Nancy Reynolds and Malcolm McCormick (2003) describe postmodern dance as a form that extended well beyond what had formerly been thought of as dance before the 1960s, embracing an array of ideas and strategies borrowed from film, music, painting, literature, the emerging field of movement therapy, and themes from various social movements. The two authors added that postmodern dance was a serious investigation into the nature of dance through the use of a process of joint or group improvisation. The postmoderns introduced elements that were a radical departure from choreographic form and method as they were understood and accepted at the middle of the 20th century. Originally, in the 1960s, this group of experimental artists was known as the Judson Dance Theater, since they presented their first series of experimental works at Judson Memorial Church in Greenwich Village. The most important contribution of the Judson Dance Theater was their extensive exploration of the limitless possibilities for dance making so that a piece of choreography could include any movement, human body, or method (Banes 2001).

Postmodern choreographers experimented with the elements of dance form and rejected the idea that a dance had to communicate a message. They were not interested in creating dances by focusing on methods developed by the choreographers who preceded them. Like many of the visual artists and composers of their era, they were intent on exploring new ground. Among their accomplishments, these innovative dance artists broadened the range of movement used in their dances; changed the traditional method of choreographic order, sequence, and timing; often worked with dancers who had various levels and types of training; danced in unique and sometimes unusual environments; incorporated aspects of technical theater or mixed media into their works; explored the use of various kinds of accompaniment; altered their dancers' relationship with the audience; and changed the traditional dance costume (McDonagh 1990). Another favorite postmodern theme, particularly in the work of Robert Dunn, was to strip movement down to one thing—a strategy that paralleled ideas used in **minimalist** sculpture (Banes 2001).

In the last quarter of the 20th century, choreographers embraced a variety of shifting trends. According to Reynolds and McCormick (2003), the postmoderns had reached and sometimes passed certain boundaries, and there was a return to emotion, story telling, clever tricks, and a high level of skill and even athleticism in the dances being created. These trends were demonstrated in the gymnastics and dramatic dances of Pilobolus; the despairing and extremely slow-moving works of Eiko and Koma; the energized, repetitive, and hypnotizing style of Molissa Fenley and Laura Dean; the daring, sometimes aerial movements of Elizabeth Streb; and the fusing of movement and dance forms in the creativity of Garth Fagan and Mark Morris (Reynolds and McCormick 2003).

As a novice choreographer, you should learn to create dances following traditional methods of form and development before attempting to experiment with postmodern methods. Once you have a solid understanding of dance form and development as it existed before the 1960s, you should find it easier to experiment with some of the ideas and concepts discovered by the postmoderns.

Dance by Chance

One postmodern method of choreography, known as dance by chance, was first used by well-known dancer and choreographer Merce Cunningham. Dance by chance is a **nontraditional** choreographic method based on the idea that there are no prescribed movement materials or orders for a series of actions. In dances developed by **chance,** the choreographer gives up some control and allows chance methods to determine the content or organization of the work. Sometimes chance methods such as a throw of dice are used in selecting movements for a dance or in giving order to the movements in a piece. Chance methods employed by Cunningham included tossing a coin to determine movement order; preparing a chart of possible movements and tossing a coin to determine which movements would be in a dance; and assigning particular movements to specific dancers but allowing the dancers to choose the speed, order, or frequency of performance of the actions (Anderson 1997). You can learn to use chance as part of your creative process by exploring some of the suggestions for developing your skills.

You'll notice that in the sections that follow, the exercises are arranged from simple to more complex. Suggestions for improvisation are included after those for exploration.

Developing Your Skills

DANCE BY CHANCE

1. Have your dancers learn a movement sequence. Then experiment with use of stage space by having the dancers begin the same movements at different points in the space. Use chance to select the area in which each dancer begins.

2. Accompaniment can also provide an element of chance. Have your dancers perform several movement sequences to different pieces of music. After you experience the effect of different musical selections, choose the one you like best.

3. Choreographers also use chance to determine the order of an entire section in a dance. Let each dancer practice the same set of movement sequences, and then arbitrarily designate the individual sequence each dancer is to perform. Have each dancer begin moving at an arbitrary point during this section of the dance. Change the order of the movement sequences. Look at how the dancers relate in the stage space, and select the order or arrangement of sequences that appeals to you for this section.

4. Write the names or descriptions of several movements and body positions on different pieces of paper—for example, walk, hop, sit, and stand. Put the pieces of paper into an arbitrary order, and decide how many times you want to perform each movement. Perform this chance sequence by connecting the separate movements with appropriate transitional movements. Devise variations of the chance sequence by altering the movement elements of space, time, energy, and shape. You could also have your dancers choose the pieces of paper and have them determine the order of the movements and the number of repetitions of each movement or pose in the sequence.

5. Cunningham constructed charts listing various movement combinations and then selected the order of the patterns to be performed by tossing coins onto the charts (Charlip 1992). Try experimenting with this method of chance determination.

6. Another chance method is to change the order of a dance using games or signals. Here the choreographer sets up a situation in which the actions of one dancer trigger movement in other dancers, producing an action–reaction scenario. According to McDonagh (1990), Deborah Hay used the game concept in her dance titled *Ten*. In this piece she had two poles onstage—one vertical and one horizontal. When the group leader used the horizontal pole, the rest of the group was expected to respond by copying the leader's stance. Use of the vertical pole was the signal for the group to form a chain. Practice making up a series of instructions or signals that determine the sequence of movements in your dance.

Pedestrian Movement

Pedestrian, or ordinary, movement is another device used in some postmodern choreography. Banes (1993) records that in *Proxy,* Steve Paxton created a slow-moving dance in four sections for three dancers. Movements in this piece included walking, carrying, and standing; in addition, the dancers drank a glass of liquid and ate a piece of fruit. Try experimenting with pedestrian movements in the following exercises.

Developing Your Skills

PEDESTRIAN MOVEMENT

1. Using chance methods, select a series of pedestrian movements and put them in an arbitrary order. Try as many variations of those movements as you can think of.

2. Broaden your scope of pedestrian actions by thinking about categories of everyday actions. These might include tasks (hammering, sweeping), daily activities (brushing your teeth, eating, sitting), or typical sport actions (baseball swing,

tennis serve, basketball throw). See how many ways you can perform each of the movements, and then link the movements together in a sequence.

3. Choreograph several different movement sequences based solely on pedestrian actions. Link the pedestrian actions with transitional movements, such as traditional locomotor steps. Try varying the locomotors used as transitions to see how using different locomotors affects each pattern.

4. Choreograph a combination of traditional dance movements, and interject some action of a pedestrian nature at intervals.

Alteration of Timing and Repetition

Timing is one of the elements of dance movement. Many of the postmodern choreographers altered the normal sense of timing or used repetitive actions as a way of discovering new dance structures. Laura Dean choreographed many works with a minimalist approach by relying on sustained actions, a mathematical progression of counts, and an ongoing steady pulse accompanied by voice, clapping, or occasional arrangements played on instruments. In her *Circle Dance,* ten dancers moved in four concentric circles while continuously whirling at a high speed (Reynolds and McCormick 2003).

Developing Your Skills

ALTERATION OF TIMING AND REPETITION

1. Try doing a dance movement more slowly or faster than normal. See what the movement feels and looks like when you perform it at an exceptionally slow rate.

2. Choose one movement—a turn, in this example. Begin to turn, altering one aspect of the turn at specific intervals. One suggestion is to change the level of the turn every 10 counts. Think of other ways to alter the repeated movement.

3. Use mathematical concepts to speed up or slow down the movement. Multiply or divide the tempo, or add or subtract counts from specific movement patterns.

4. Walk in a set floor pattern. (This should be a pattern that can be repeated many times, such as a square or circle.) Change the direction of your walking at specific intervals, and then move through the same floor pattern using a different locomotor step.

5. Try these explorations with both large and small groups.

Group Size and Technical Level

The nature and size of a group can do much to affect the dynamics in a dance. The postmodern dancers often incorporated extremely large groups in their choreography or used groups that included dancers of varied technical abilities. Deborah Hay and Meredith Monk, for example, worked with large groups, while Rudy Perez used the team concept in some of his works (McDonagh 1990). These choreographers usually developed such dances from simple rather than complex movement materials, since both trained and untrained dancers performed in them.

Developing Your Skills

GROUP SIZE AND TECHNICAL LEVEL

1. You can experiment with groups of various sizes. Construct a short movement sequence and teach it to one or two dancers. View the movement pattern, and then add more dancers to the group. Continue the addition of dancers to determine the effect produced by small and large groups when they perform the same pattern.

2. The use of dancers of varied technical levels can also introduce a unique creative problem. You could try using two different movement vocabularies for the two different groups. The lay dancers would do simple movements and pedestrian actions, whereas the trained dancers could perform more complex and traditional dance movements. It would also be interesting to have the untrained performers move in place while the trained dancers travel around them. Experiment with the possibilities by changing the stage area used by each of the two groups or by altering the point at which each group begins to move.

Unusual Environments

Postmodern choreographers have often danced in unusual environments, such as on the altar of a church, in the street, or in an art museum. Meredith Monk also enjoyed doing works that evolved from and were inspired by different environments. *Juice,* choreographed by Monk, included 85 performers and began at New York's Guggenheim Museum where the audience was guided to various locations for viewing different stages of the performance; other parts of the dance were performed over the period of a month at different places in the city (Reynolds and McCormick 2003). In figure 2.20, Monk's dancers are performing *Vessel,* another of her site-based works. I remember seeing Monk's company perform at the Water Gardens, a series of large fountains in Fort Worth. During the performance, it was necessary for the audience to follow the dancers from one of the fountains to the next one with the help of a map.

Photo by Monica Moseley. From The New York Public Library for the Performing Arts, Jerome Robbins Dance Division, Astor, Lenox and Tilden Foundations.

Figure 2.20   Meredith Monk, The House at Goddard College in *Vessel.*

Developing Your Skills

UNUSUAL ENVIRONMENTS

1. Create an experimental environment in the dance studio by placing or suspending props such as hoops, chairs, boxes, and scooters at points around the room. Other props, large enough to hide one or several dancers, could include a screen or piano. Have your dancers discover many actions by relating to the objects in various ways and by reacting to each other. Stimulate imagination by having your dancers move over, under, around, and through the objects in the dance space (see figure 2.21). After the improvisation has continued for a while, select some of the most effective sequences, and set them in a short dance.

Figure 2.21 Many different objects can be used in creating a changed studio environment for improvisation.

2. Extend the movement possibilities in the preceding exercise by having your dancers copy or relate to the movements of others as they continue to improvise.

3. Check your campus or dance building for other spaces that could provide a new environment for improvisations.

4. You can also discover new dance environments by exploring a bare stage or by using the theater-in-the-round concept.

5. On a warm day, go outside and improvise. Have your dancers concentrate on the objects in this new setting, and then ask them to move over, under, around, and through the objects.

6. Choreographers have also used slides and other kinds of projections to alter the performance setting. Project a slide on a bare wall and watch your dancers move in front of the projection. (Slides of modern art are effective for this exercise because the projection contains large designs or blocks of color without realistic images.) Notice how the projection changes and takes on a life of its own as the dancers move in front of it.

7. Project a computer-generated image on the wall or a blank screen and have your dancers move in front of it.

Accompaniment

Accompaniment has an important effect on the kind of choreography you create. The post-modern dancers used many different and often unusual forms of accompaniment. In some of her early works, Twyla Tharp danced in silence or to the accompaniment of the rhythmic sounds of nature. Yvonne Rainer used the human voice and the amplified sounds of her own body as accompaniment (McDonagh 1990).

Developing Your Skills

ACCOMPANIMENT

1. Try improvising to various sounds of nature, such as the wind, running water, or crickets. (Before you begin to move, concentrate on the unique quality of the sounds, trying to experience them in terms of the six qualities of movement discussed earlier in the chapter.)

2. Make your own accompaniment by recording words, nonsense syllables, or the sounds of walking on various surfaces. (Walking on gravel, for example, creates an interesting crunching sound.) Try improvising with each new form of accompaniment.

3. Alter the pitch and quality of the sounds in the preceding exercise by changing the speed of your tape recorder, or record the sounds at a different speed so they take on another quality.

4. Have your group of dancers move around the space while making body sounds or rhythmic patterns by clapping, stamping, or slapping their bodies. Encourage the dancers to try different rhythms and to copy the patterns of other dancers from time to time.

5. Select five or six names or words that fit a category. Categories could be colors, flowers, cars, and so forth. Have one of the dancers in your group pick one of the words and say it loudly in a way that suggests a movement quality such as sustained or percussive. The dancer should also move while saying the word. Immediately encourage the other dancers to respond to the first dancer by saying the same word and moving as well. Try to keep the action going by altering the quality of movement and vocalization. (When movement begins to quiet down, another dancer should be ready to call out a second word from the category to initiate the process again. In this exercise, it's important for the dancers to be aware of each other so that they can respond to and play off the sounds and actions of others in the group.)

Group Interaction

The proscenium theater creates a performer–audience relationship in which the two entities remain separate. The edges of the top and sides of the proscenium arch and the floor of the theater form a picture frame that surrounds the performance area and separates it from the audience. The postmodern choreographers challenged this traditional separation of performer and audience by having dancers perform in the audience area or by having them enter the stage from the **house.** Some of the new choreographers even tried having the dancers pick up sounds or gestures made by audience members.

Developing Your Skills

GROUP INTERACTION

1. Have your group begin this improvisation by moving freely around the dance space while other dancers are the audience. Then suggest that the dancers initiate changes by copying the movements and gestures of the observers. The changes could occur at random or on a signal from someone inside or outside the group. (Accompaniment may help initiate movement changes.)

2. Dancers can produce variations in movement by manipulating the movement elements or by reacting to the actions of the other dancers.

3. Begin with an empty dance space. Place your dancers at various points along the periphery of this space, and have the dancers enter and exit the dance space when they feel ready to do so. Keep the action going by encouraging the dancers to relate to each other while they move within the dance area. (The idea is that there is an exchange between performers and audience, because the same dancer is both an audience member and a performer, but at different times.)

4. Try the previous improvisation using unusual movements during entrances and exits. You might have the dancers roll, crawl, or slide their bodies into the dance space.

Structured Improvisation

The **structured improvisation** is another postmodern idea similar to the game concept. Here, the choreographer uses certain criteria to determine where and how the dancers move in the performance space. An example of a structured improvisation is one proposed by Barbara Dilley (1981) in which the choreographer instructs the dancers to move only in a circular and counterclockwise pathway using select movements such as walking, running, crawling, and standing. The dancers are also told to be sensitive to each other by picking up the movement of other dancers when it feels right. Dilley based another structured improvisation on spatial corridors. In this improvisation, the performers are instructed to move across the room in several selected corridors of the dance space; the kinds of movement to be used are again prescribed. Dancers who cross the entire space must exit and reenter through a different corridor.

Developing Your Skills

STRUCTURED IMPROVISATION

1. Limit the movements or poses to be used in this improvisation to four or five possibilities. For example, the dancers' movements could be walk, run, stand, and hop. Have your dancers move counterclockwise in a circle using only the selected movements and moving only in a circular pathway. Let the dancers do these movements in any order, and encourage them to copy the actions of other dancers from time to time.

2. Decide on how many corridors of space divide the dance studio. Then choose the four or five movements to be used to cross the space. Let your dancers move across the space while staying in the corridor that they entered. Again, encourage them to copy the actions of others from time to time, and when they exit, have them reenter the dance space in a different corridor. Allow both of these improvisations to continue for three to five minutes. Try to remember the interesting points in each improvisation, and write them down for use in a composition.

Contact Improvisation

Contact improvisation, another creative idea that has emerged, is used in the studio to discover movement and as a performance medium. Contact work is a spontaneous form drawn from functional actions performed while relating to the environment or to a moving partner. Motivation is taken from a dancer's reaction to being in contact with another moving body and from learning to take and receive impulses from another. Contact improvisation is very spontaneous, since the point of contact between bodies is not predetermined; rather, it is allowed to evolve and progress naturally. Often the weight of one dancer's body is supported by another. Sessions in contact improvisation should be conducted with care, and participants should employ mechanically efficient movement techniques. Dancers must know how to relax when falling, roll when meeting the floor, bear weight safely, and catch themselves protectively yet be able to keep the energy going. Contact improvisation challenged many assumptions in dance and provided a spontaneous atmosphere of indistinct beginnings and endings; it was motivated by the momentum of contact between ever-changing parts of the body (Foster 2001).

Developing Your Skills

CONTACT IMPROVISATION

1. You can play with contact improvisation. Begin in a position in which your body weight is supported by another dancer, and start to move slowly, being aware of how movement of both participants alters body contact, weight, and body shape. Notice the point at which one body supports the other and how support and contact change as body shapes change.

2. Try the preceding exercise while you and your partner move in space rather than remain in one area doing axial movements.

3. As a variation on contact improvisation, stand facing a partner. (You and your partner should be about the same height and weight.) Grasp both of your partner's forearms with a good grip, and pull away so that you and your partner counterbalance one another. Continue counterbalancing, but change body shape by taking one foot off the floor or by changing levels. See how many movements you can create while you continue to counterbalance your partner (see figure 2.22).

Figure 2.22 The dancers are counterbalancing.

4. Try contact improvisation in a larger group once you have practiced with one person. Take care to move slowly and cautiously throughout this process.

Extending Dance Making With Technology

The combination of dance and **technology** is not new to the 21st century. Dance performances have always required the use of some form of technology. When ballet and other forms of theater were first presented on indoor stages, the lighting involved some kind of combustible material in the form of oil lamps, candles, gas jets, or a mixture of lime and other chemicals

(Swift 2004). Thus, the technology of the day was used for lighting the performance area, and the physical strength of many stage hands was needed for lowering or hoisting and pushing or pulling scenery and even performers on and off the stage.

With the advent of electricity in the 20th century, performances became less dangerous and more mechanized, and fewer theaters burned to the ground. Electricity also lent itself to more elaborate lighting effects as more refined lighting instruments and control systems were invented. The new technology also affected the accompaniment for dance through the use of electronic sound scores. By the end of the 20th century, computers and other new forms of technology were radically altering the nature of dance both in the studio and on the stage. Some of these technological innovations are relatively simple to use, whereas others are complex and require a high level of computer skill and more than a beginner's command of multiple forms of technology. The important point is that whether simple or complex, 21st-century technology in its various forms can be used to extend the creativity of choreographers.

Aerial Dance

Aerial dance is one of the technological innovations that has become popular on the dance scene since its inception in 1976 through the work of pioneer Terry Sendgraff in the San Francisco Bay Area. In aerial dance, the performers move through aerial choreography while suspended above the stage floor; often ground-based movement performed at floor level is blended with aerial work. The low-flying trapeze, aerial hoop, aerial fabric, bungee cords, and rope and harness are some of the apparatus used in aerial performances. Aerial performances have also included vertical dance in which the performers move in different directions on a vertical wall or dance on stilts (see figure 2.23).

Photo: Robert Goldhamer, Frequent Flyer Productions.

Figure 2.23   An aerial dance performed at a festival staged by Frequent Flyers Productions, Boulder, Colorado.

Developing Your Skills

AERIAL DANCE

1. You can get some idea of what it is like to create aerial dances by visiting a playground or park near your home. There, you can experiment with the movement possibilities when you lie, sit, or stand on a swing.

2. What about creating movement while riding on a merry-go-round? What are the possible ways in which you can position and move your body while riding on this and other playground equipment?

Using Computer-Generated Images in Dance

Many of us have seen dance performances in which colored images were used to provide a background for the dancers. Recently, computers have been used to create such images, which are projected onto the cyc (short for **cyclorama,** the background) during a dance performance. This means that background imagery used in a dance is not limited to designs or patterns sold by lighting companies in the form of **gobos** (masks placed at the gate of a spotlight to project a pattern by blocking out portions of the light beam), but can be created anew to fit the intent of choreography.

I used the computer-generated approach in a dance called *Faces of the Goddess* in which the background images were created by Anna Ursyn, a **computer graphics** professor at the University of Northern Colorado. Ursyn created the images after she and I discussed the meanings of the various sections of the work (see figure 2.24).

Image by Anna Ursyn created in Fortran, "Report from Colorado."

Figure 2.24 A computer-generated design created for *Faces of the Goddess,* choreographed by Sandra Minton.

I saw a similar approach used in a *Nutcracker* production presented by the David Taylor Dance Theatre. In this production, the images were projected onto the cyc from a position in front of the stage. One interesting image was a clock on which the hands moved around the face of the clock to show that time was passing. The use of computer-generated imagery has enabled the company to take the *Nutcracker* production on the road without hauling cumbersome sets from one location to another (see figure 2.25).

Another Colorado choreographer, Judy Bejarano (2002), used a similar approach in her evening-length dance piece titled *This Speaking Body*. In this work, text, still images, video, and **animations** were projected onto the cyc to support what was happening onstage. Thus, the projected text and imagery supplemented the meaning of the movement, dialogue, and accompaniment performed live so that the two components became an integrated whole. The computer technology-PowerPoint was used in creating the text and images that were played by means of rear projection (see figure 2.26).

Photo: Robert Goldhamer.
Choreography: David Taylor.
Background Image Design: Jonathan Scott-McKean.

Figure 2.25 A computer-generated background created by Jonathan Scott-McKean for the David Taylor Dance Theatre's *Nutcracker*.

Photo courtesy of Richard Finkelstein.
Photos from "This Speaking Body," choreographed and directed by Judy Bejarano while in residence at Colorado State University.
Multimedia Design: M. Barrett Cleveland.

Figure 2.26 A cyc projection and live performer in *This Speaking Body*, a theater and dance work created by Judy Bejarano, Director of Impact Dance. Work was performed at Colorado State University at Fort Collins.

A different approach to technology has been used by a number of choreographers to create the actual movements or the organization of actions in a dance. Choreographers Merce Cunningham and William Forsythe have both used computers to create or arrange movements. In Cunningham's case, the **computer program** DanceForms was used for creating about one third of the movements in a work titled *Trackers* (see figure 2.27, *a* and *b*). LifeForms, the original version of DanceForms, was created at Simon Fraser University; these computer programs produce three-dimensional computer-generated figures that can be altered and manipulated to sketch out movement ideas in space and time (Schiphorst 1992). A number of other models have been used to depict the human figure on a computer screen, including joined prisms, stick figures, bubble men, and sausage men (Gray 1989). At a National Dance Education Organization Conference, Ilene Fox, Rhonda Ryman, and Tom Calvert (2002) described how they were building a bridge between the computer-generated figures and **Labanotation,** a system of written symbols used in recording dances. To build such a bridge, the team used computers as an interface between movement recorded using LabanWriter, a computerized version of Labanotation, and the computer-animated figures.

Developing Your Skills

COMPUTER-GENERATED IMAGES

1. Select a painting created by a 20th-century artist that you admire. The painting can be fairly realistic or it can be **abstract.** Photograph the painting; once you have the photo, scan it into your computer. If you have a digital camera, you can simply load your photo onto your computer from the camera and then copy it to a CD. When this CD is read by a laptop computer connected to a projector, you will have an enlarged image of the painting. As you look at this projected

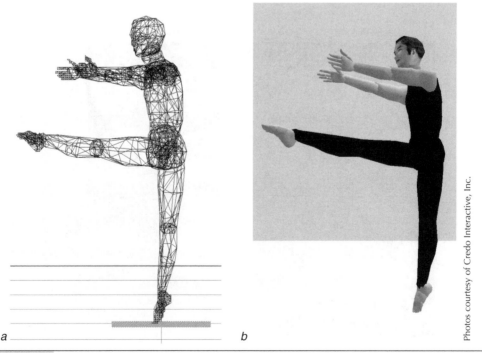

a   b

Photos courtesy of Credo Interactive, Inc.

Figure 2.27   *(a)* Version of computer-generated figure used by Cunningham to create some of the movements in *Trackers;* and *(b)* the most recent version of a DanceForms figure created by Credo Interactive, Vancouver, Canada.

image, select one shape, one line, and one color as your inspiration for creating movement. Next, focus on how you feel about the shape, line, and color you have selected. By focusing on your feelings, you are focusing on your response to the inspiration, which is the second step in the framework for creating movement presented in chapter 1. As you focus on your feeling response, begin to improvise and create movement. The last step is to combine your movements together to create a sequence. Have someone watch as you perform your movement sequence in front of the projected painting. How did the person feel about merging your movements with the projected image?

2. Think of several word phrases that describe your feelings about the painting. Then focus on those words and improvise again. Did you find that the feeling-oriented words caused you to move differently than your feelings about the shape, line, and color from the painting did? The words you just used as an inspiration can also be inserted in a PowerPoint document and projected onto a screen to serve as a background for your movements.

3. If you have a graphics program on your computer or if you know someone who does, create your own abstract design that captures your feelings about the painting. The computer-generated design could also be projected as a background for your movement.

Using the Internet to Choreograph

For the brave of heart, the **Internet** can be used as a dance performance medium. Real-time processing of dance performances at various sites in the world have been coordinated through the integrated use of video, communication, and Internet technologies (Birringer 2003 and 2004). Such a **teleperformance** was created at the International Dance and Technology Conference (IDAT) in 1999. In that performance, the Australian dance group Company in Space staged *Escape Velocity* in which two dancers—one in Melbourne and one at Arizona State University in Tempe—performed the same dance simultaneously. Two video cameras and two projectors were linked by a direct online connection so that the audiences at each site could see both dancers—one who was live and one who was projected on a large screen. A slight delay in transmission between the two sites created a type of dialogue at times between the dancer who was physically present and the dancing image, or virtual dancer, transmitted via the Internet (see figure 2.28).

In a similar vein, an educational project brought dance students together from three countries—Britain, Portugal, and the United States (Popat 2002). In this project, the three groups of students used video and text messages transmitted via the Internet to jointly create a dance. The ultimate goal was to use the Internet to perform the entire dance simultaneously at the different sites. Unfortunately, this goal was not fully realized at the end of the project.

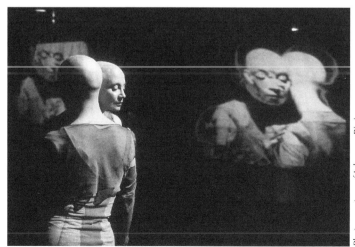

Photo courtesy of Johannes Birringer.
Hellen Sky (Arizona IDAT) and Louise Taube (Australia) performing ESCAPE VELOCITY, a telematic Company in Space performance.

Figure 2.28 Hellen Sky and Louise Taube performing *Escape Velocity,* a telematic Company in Space performance staged at the 1999 IDAT Conference.

Developing Your Skills

USING THE INTERNET

1. Find a site on the Internet that depicts dancers who are moving rather than still. You can find such a site by going to the Google search engine and typing in "OK Go Treadmill Dance." Watch the performance of the dancers several times and then simultaneously perform one of the movement sequences you see on your computer. Were you able to dance along with the dancers on your computer?

2. Vary some of the movements in the sequence you selected from that site. Remember, you can vary movements by changing the use of space, time, energy, and body shape.

3. Using only words, describe the movements you created in the previous exercise, and e-mail the description to a dancer friend who lives near you. Once your friend has read your movement description, he or she should be able to perform your movements. Check out your friend's performance of the movements by watching him or her perform them live or on video. Did the movements look the same as those you created?

4. You can also use still photos to choreograph via the Internet. To do this, have someone take several photos of you as you perform the previous movement sequence. Scan the photos onto your computer and e-mail them to a friend, suggesting that he or she create a movement sequence based on the series of still photos. Finally, watch your friend perform the movements created. Did the movements performed by your friend look like the movements you had created originally?

Virtual Choreography

Choreography in which a **virtual dancer** performs with a live dancer onstage has also been produced. One way to accomplish this is to have a video camera set up onstage so that an image of the live performers is projected onto the cyc during the performance, creating an interplay between the live dancers and their projected images. This technique was used in a concert by Michael O'Banion, director of dance at Denver School of the Arts. The Ririe-Woodbury Dance Company has used a slightly different approach by combining projected images of previously videotaped dancers with a live performance onstage (see figure 2.29).

Photo by Fred Hayes.
Photo courtesy of Ririe-Woodbury Dance Company.

Figure 2.29 Members of the Ririe-Woodbury Dance Company in *Nowhere Bird,* a work in which live performers and images of videotaped dancers merge in one work.

Motion capture, however, is a much different method of combining the performance of live and virtual dancers. With the use of motion capture, a live dancer performs selected movements with reflective markers attached to his or her body while a video camera records those actions. Then, a computer is used to change the spatial coordinates, or locations, of the markers in space into a series of images that is like an electronic double of the dancer's actions (Hodges 1995). Paul Kaiser and Shelley Eshkar have used motion capture to produce a virtual dancing image of Bill T. Jones in a work called *Ghostcatching* (see figure 2.30). During the production of *Ghostcatching,* the recordings went through several stages, or transformations, that resulted in animations of the original video recordings of Jones (Dils 2002).

While *Ghostcatching* appears as a solo ethereal moving image, *Biped,* a work created by Cunningham, combined similar images created through motion capture with the performance of live dancers (see figure 2.31). *Biped* begins with Cunningham's dancers performing a series of solos, but as the work develops,

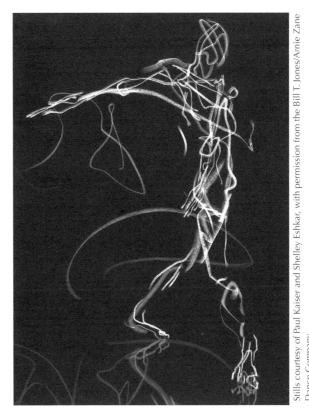

Stills courtesy of Paul Kaiser and Shelley Eshkar, with permission from the Bill T. Jones/Arnie Zane Dance Company.

Figure 2.30 A digital image of Bill T. Jones in *Ghostcatching,* created by Paul Kaiser and Shelley Eshkar. The image was created through the use of motion capture.

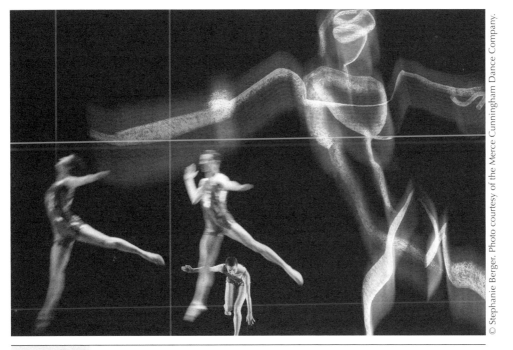

© Stephanie Berger. Photo courtesy of the Merce Cunningham Dance Company.

Figure 2.31 *Biped* is a work by Merce Cunningham in which digital images and live dancers merge.

digital projections created by Kaiser and Eshkar and the lighting of Aaron Copp immerse the performers in an ever-changing environment of motion capture–generated images and lighting (Dils 2002).

The electronic recordings made with motion capture were also used for a performance by the Atlanta Ballet. To help create this ballet, choreographed by Lisa de Ribere Larkin and titled *Non Sequitur,* a group of computer scientists videotaped a male dancer using motion capture. Then, an electronic double was built based on the male dancer's movements. The double was projected onto an onstage screen so that the virtual dancer and his real-life partner could perform a duet (Hodges 1995).

Developing Your Skills

VIRTUAL CHOREOGRAPHY

1. Locate a copy of the DanceForms program. Maneuver the virtual onscreen figure so that it is performing one of the movement sequences you created in the previous Developing Your Skills section.

2. Change the use of space, time, energy, or body shape in the movements of the virtual figure. Compare this new sequence to the movement sequence performed in exploration 1.

3. Try creating a short movement sequence from scratch by using the virtual figure instead of moving or improvising with your own body.

Other Audio and Optical Technology Uses

Various other forms of technology, such as **audio suits, optical suits,** and **intelligent stages,** have been used in creating **interactive** dance works that evolve in real time. An interactive performance environment is alive only when a body is moving in it (Povall 1998). For example, in a performance by the dance company Troika Ranch, dancer Dawn Stoppiello moved while costumed in a sensory suit called Midi-Dancer. The sensory suit was invented by Mark Coniglio (see figure 2.32). Through the MidiDancer's sensors, encoded information is sent to an off-stage computer, enabling the dancer's movements to control the dynamics and timing of music and video projections (Jackson 1999).

Photo courtesy of Steven A. Gunther.

Figure 2.32 Dawn Stoppiello of Troika Ranch dancing while wearing the MidiDancer.

Heartbeat, a duet, is another example of an interactive dance. In this work, the two dancers wore chest electrodes so that the beating of their hearts could be converted into musical tones (Wechsler 1998). The Very Nervous System, developed by David Rokeby, combines video cameras, **artificial perception,** a computer, and a **synthesizer** to create a space in which the movements of the dancers are transformed into sound, music, and video projections (Birringer 2002). While such interactive dances present a myriad of creative possibilities, they do require expensive technology and laboratory-like environments.

Lisa Marie Naugle is a dancer and choreographer who has worked extensively with computer technology and dance through the use of motion capture and two-way video conferencing. At the 1999 IDAT Conference she presented *Janus/Ghost Stories,* a work created through the use of a video-conferencing environment communicated over **broadband** networks (Naugle 2002). Naugle has also given considerable thought to the pedagogical implications of combining technology and dance. She believes that technology should be used in a way that emphasizes human intelligence. Rather than use technology in a passive way, we need to use technology in an active way that enhances human expression and extends opportunities to communicate across cultures (Naugle 1998). Used in this way, technology will not lead to disembodied dancers and dance works that are controlled wholly by computers (see figure 2.33).

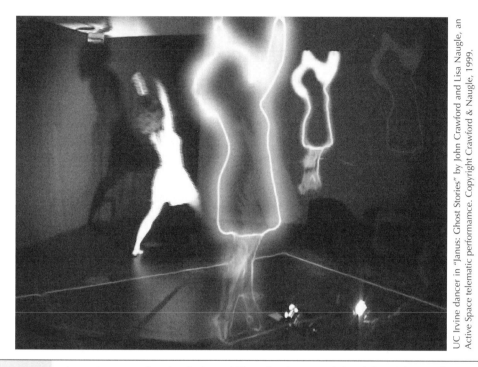

UC Irvine dancer in "Janus: Ghost Stories" by John Crawford and Lisa Naugle, an Active Space telematic performamce. Copyright Crawford & Naugle, 1999.
Contact : john.crawford@uci.edu

Figure 2.33 Laura James performing in *Janus/Ghost Stories,* a work involving video conferencing.

Developing Your Skills

AUDIO AND OPTICAL DEVICES

1. Go to the Troika Ranch site on the Internet (www.troikaranch.org) and read more about how this group has used the MidiDancer in their creative work. After reading about Troika Ranch, imagine what it would be like to perform while wearing the MidiDancer. How would wearing the MidiDancer or a similar device affect or alter your performance?

2. Think about some of the movement sequences you have created in the exercises in the Developing Your Skills sections devoted to dance and technology. How might you integrate the MidiDancer or a similar device with the performance of your movements?

3. Choreograph a new sequence of movements that is created with the MidiDancer or the Very Nervous System in mind. As you improvise, think about how you could extend the impact of your movements by using such forms of technology.

Developing the Design and Shape of Your Dance

From reading the preceding section, you should be able to understand that computer technology and dance can be partnered in many ways. Images have been used as backgrounds and as virtual dancing partners during live performances. Computer programs such as LifeForms and DanceForms have also been used in lieu of live dancers to create movement and make dances. In addition, a number of interfaces between live dance performers and computers have been created with devices such as MidiDancer and the Very Nervous System. Video conferencing via the Internet has been used as a dance performance venue as well.

PRACTICAL APPLICATIONS

CREATE

1. Return to one of the sequences of movement you created in response to figure 1.10, *a* or *b* (page 27) and create a spatial variation of that sequence. Creating a spatial variation of the sequence means that you would change it in terms of direction, size, level, or use of focus.

2. Create a second variation of the same movement sequence, but this time change your use of energy or timing.

3. Create a third variation of the same sequence by changing your use of body shape.

4. If you were working with a group of dancers, it would also be possible to create added variations of your movement sequence by creating group shapes or by having your dancers move in unison, opposition, or sequence at different times throughout your piece. Imagine how you could use one or more of these choreographic devices to manipulate the movement sequence you created in response to figure 1.10, *a* or *b*.

5. The placement of dancers in specific areas of the stage, their facing, and their position in relation to other dancers is also important. Imagine how you could most optimally position your dancers onstage as they perform one of the movement sequences you created in response to figure 1.10, *a* or *b*.

6. Select one of the choreographic ideas from the postmodern dance era that you think you would like to use in a dance. Explain how that choreographic technique works, and then describe how you would transform the choreographic device into movement.

7. Select one of the choreographic ideas from the postmodern dance era that you would never use in your own dance. Explain how that choreographic technique works, and then describe how, in particular, you feel about that method of making a dance. Why do you think you would use one of those choreographic ideas in your own choreography but could not see yourself using the other idea in your work?

8. Reread the "Extending Dance Making With Technology" section (pages 60-69) on how technology can be used in enhancing dance making. Explain how you would use one of the technologies described as part of the movement-creation process in your own work. As you think about the creative movement process, be sure that your use of the technology contributes to the intent or overall design of your dance; it should not be merely a decoration.

PERFORM

1. Perform each of the movement variations you created in the preceding exercises. Which of the variations is the easiest to perform? Which one is the most difficult to perform? Why did you identify one of those sequences as easy to perform and the other one as more difficult?

2. Which of the movement variations best fits the sculpture that served as your creative inspiration?

3. Perform at least two of the movement variations you have created. Compare or contrast how each one felt in your body. Make sure that you describe in what way they felt similar or different.

REFLECT

1. Watch a video of a dance created by a well-known choreographer. The dance you observe should be one in which there is a feeling-oriented relationship between the dancers or in which the dancers portray different characters in a tale or story. Were specific movements or movement sequences repeated in the dance?

2. When movements or sequences were repeated, were they varied in any way? Be specific about how the variations were created.

3. Watch the same video again and observe and then describe how the dancers are positioned and moved around the dance space. In addition, describe how the dancers relate to each other in the stage space. Do you think that the choreographer's use of stage area and the relationship between the dancers contributed to the meaning or effectiveness of the dance?

4. Consider the same choreography you just viewed and observe and then describe how the dancers' facial expressions and facing contributed to the meaning they portrayed.

5. View the same choreography a fourth time, but this time look at the choreographer's use of groupings of dancers and negative space between dancers. Describe the use of groupings of dancers and negative space. Do you think that the use of groupings and negative space contributed to the success of the dance?

6. What are the differences between unison, sequence, and opposition? Did you observe any use of unison, sequence, or opposition in the choreography you just viewed? Do you think the use of unison, sequence, or opposition added to the effectiveness of the dance?

7. Stand in front of a mirror and perform two of the movement variations you created in response to the sculpture inspiration pictured in figure 1.10, *a* or *b*. Then compare the visual aspects of each movement sequence. For example, did the movement sequences look different in terms of body shape or direction?

8. Make a video as you perform the same two movement variations. Is your impression of the sequences different than when you watched yourself perform them in the mirror?

Choreography Challenge

The following challenge is a continuation of the challenge in chapter 1. Remember that at the end of chapter 1 you created movements based on an inspiration from the list on pages 5 to 7.

Creating Movement Variations for Your Dance

- Movement manipulation is one of the choreographic techniques discussed in this chapter. You used the elements of movement—space, time, energy, and shape—in manipulating or extending movements you created through exploration and improvisation. Return to the movement sequences that you created at the end of chapter 1 and decide which of the movement elements you will use to vary those actions. Then, improvise as you focus on that element.

- Create other variations of the movement sequence by focusing on the other movement elements.

- Using the process of improvisation, create additional movement sequences and possible variations based on the same inspiration.

Visualizing Movement Arrangements and Relationships

- Again, focus on your inspiration and decide what ideas or feelings you want to communicate through your dance. Begin to think about where in your dance you will include the various movement sequences you have created. For example, would a particular sequence be at the beginning, middle, or end of your dance?

- Give some thought to where in the stage space the movements will be performed and how the dancers can relate to each other. Would one sequence be better performed by a soloist or by a group?

- What relationships or changing relationships do you see taking place in your dance? Do you think the use of unison, opposition, or sequence would be appropriate for any part of your dance? What about the use of group shapes or negative space?

- Could you use any of the choreographic techniques from postmodern dance or any form of computer technology in your work?

Working With Your Dancers

- Begin with one of the movement sequences or its variation that you created in the previous exercises. Teach the sequence to your dancers and watch as they perform it. Then decide whether you want to arrange the movements in a different way and whether those movements should be performed in a different stage area.

- Continue to teach your dancers the other movement sequences you have created. You may want to leave those sequences as you originally created them or alter them in terms of the techniques suggested in this chapter.

- Watch your dancers perform the movement sequences and begin to decide on an order or progression in which each would be performed in your dance.

- If necessary, return to your inspiration and create additional movements or movement sequences. Teach those movements to your dancers and think about where you will include the movements in your work.

3

Identifying Choreographic Form

Any creative work, dance included, exists within a **form** that is shaped from the inspiration or **intent** of the work. Giving form to your dance occurs after you have discovered some of the movements. In terms of the framework presented in chapter 1, finding form happens after you begin to transform your inspiration into movement. Since the framework for creating a dance is circular rather than linear, however, giving form to your work may be interrupted by new movement discoveries or new arrangements of movement. The dance phrase and criteria of effective form are described in this chapter, followed by a discussion of how you can use these techniques to shape a dance. Common dance forms are introduced along with explanations to help you understand literal, abstraction, and nonliteral choreographic methods and the concept of style. This chapter concludes with advice on selecting appropriate subjects for your choreography, working through the developmental stages of dance making, and putting finishing touches on your work. The materials in this chapter relate to the second dance standard, which states that students should understand choreographic principles, processes, and structures (National Dance Association 1996), because they are maps for forming your dance. By exploring some of the suggestions for movement phrasing and dance form, you will begin to get a sense of what these aspects of the choreographic craft look like and how they feel in your body. Your sense of dance phrasing and form will gradually become internalized, leaving you free to create movement phrases and form dances in your own personal way.

Many people not trained in the choreographic craft are nevertheless capable of identifying a successful dance. These people intuitively know an effective work when they see it. What they can't do, however, is analyze why a dance is successful or describe what distinguishes an effective piece of choreography from a less effective work. In these pages we consider some of the elements involved in designing a dance—one that creates an illusion of being larger than life and that conveys a sense of magic and wonder.

Choreographic Form and Development

An effective piece of choreography has a special quality that makes the observer want to get involved. The observer is lifted from the theater seat and transported during the performance.

One of the criteria of an effective dance is that it has a shape, or form—a form that progresses through time from the beginning to the end of the choreography. In learning how to choreograph, therefore, you need to develop a sense of how to give overall form to a composition. One description of the development of a dance is that the choreography has a beginning, middle, and end. The choreographer learns to shape a dance so that each of the parts is essential and fits together with the others to form a whole. In learning to compose a dance, you will develop your ability to choose an appropriate beginning, middle, and end that relate to the form and feeling of the whole choreography.

Later, you can use video to help in an analysis of your own dances. Through the use of video, you can stand outside a dance and view form and development with a critical eye.

As you choreograph, be aware of the total structure of your dance as it evolves; resist the tendency to get lost or completely involved in any single movement or sequence of movements. In other words, learn to stand outside the work and maintain a mental picture of the **overall development** of the dance.

Observing and Responding

EXPERIENCE IN ACTION

The following exercises allow you to observe and explore choreographic form so that you can begin to recognize it in others' works and use it in your own. Record your thoughts and drawings in a journal so that you can organize your ideas and also look back on what you've learned for future reference.

1. Watch a video of a well-known choreographer's work. Notice how the dance develops. See if you can identify the beginning, middle, and ending sections in the dance. (See appendix A for a list of distributors of dance videos.) To understand the overall form of the work chosen, use your own words to write a description of how the choreographer developed the dance.

2. Make a simple visual diagram based on your written analysis of the work in the preceding exercise (see figure 3.1).

3. Compare your analysis of the choreography with an analysis of the same work made by a classmate. Note how your analysis may differ from the one made by the other person.

Figure 3.1   The two drawings represent the overall form of two different dances.

Adapted from L.A. Blom and L.T. Chaplin, 1982, *The intimate act of choreography* (Pittsburgh, PA: University of Pittsburgh Press).

4. Compare the form and development of two different pieces of choreography. Try to draw a diagram of each.

The Phrase

Many smaller pieces of movement make up the overall shape or development of a dance composition. The smaller units of a dance are known as phrases and can be likened to the phrases that make up sentences in a written composition. Blom and Chaplin (1982) describe the phrase as the smallest unit of form in the whole dance. Musician Robert Kaplan (2002), who has worked with dancers for many years, wrote that phrases are small units, and one unit follows another unit to create a larger entity; in speech a phrase can be a grouping of words spoken in one breath. Beginning choreographers need to learn movement phrasing—an ability that can be acquired with the use of both the visual and **kinesthetic sense.**

A phrase must have a sense of development. You need to understand how others have used phrasing as you develop a kinesthetic awareness of the phrasing in your own work. One example of a phrase is a unit of movement marked by an impulse of energy that grows, builds, and finds a conclusion and then flows easily and naturally into the next movement phrase in the dance. A phrase could also have a different form based on other uses of energy so that the separate movements connect in a more abrupt manner or are developed by arbitrarily linking movements together. When linking movements arbitrarily, however, you will need to give thought to the way in which the movements are connected. Each of the separate movements in a phrase must be related to a common intent (Blom and Chaplin 1982). Many phrases make up a section in the choreography, and the sections together form the entire dance.

Movement phrases should vary in length and shape. When all phrases in a dance are of equal length—eight counts long, say—phrasing becomes very predictable and boring for the audience, and the dance can become monotonous. Likewise, movement phrases that all begin with an impulse of energy and end with a slow decline in that energy would have a similar shape because each would be developed in the same manner. Kaplan (2002) encourages dancers to work with less common phrase structures such as those that include 10 counts or 14 counts, although it is difficult to find accompaniment to fit such movement structures.

Dance phrasing is not always easy to understand. You might have difficulty, for instance, if you have learned dance technique or movement skills by learning **steps.** To alleviate this problem, you need to realize how movements connect and where one energy impulse ends and a new impulse begins. Some dancers have learned movement patterns that have poor transitions or no connecting link at all between the basic movements or steps. As a beginning choreographer, you should develop an awareness of the connectedness of movement and stop thinking about the steps learned in dance technique class.

Observing and Responding

EXPERIENCE IN ACTION

1. Watch a videotape of a well-known choreographer's work. Notice where the phrases begin and end. See if you can pick out the movement phrases throughout the work.

2. As you watch the video, notice where the choreographer has used recognizable steps, and try to understand how those steps are integrated into the overall development of the dance.

3. Discuss your analysis of movement phrasing with a classmate to compare your understanding of phrasing to your classmate's ideas.

4. Write down your observations in a journal.

Developing Your Skills

PHRASING

The point of these explorations is both to give you a chance to practice movement phrasing and to increase your understanding of the concept. You will develop phrases by using a number of motivations and then reinforce that understanding by doing exercises using various sensory modes. You might find a visual model, such as a drawing or diagram, to be a helpful aid in comprehension. A classmate, on the other hand, might respond to auditory cues, such as singing the rhythmic development of each phrase. Approaching phrasing, or any other concept, in various ways should increase your understanding.

Understanding Phrasing

The following explorations provide a more concrete way to understand phrasing.

1. Try performing several of the phrases that you observed in the video in the preceding explorations while chanting or singing their rhythm or development.

2. Clarify the chanting exploration with the use of a visual diagram. In such a diagram the line goes up when the movement or energy goes up, drops down when the movement goes down, becomes shorter for faster movement, and is absent to accompany pauses in the phrase. Create visual diagrams for several of your movement phrases (see figure 3.2).

Figure 3.2   The two drawings represent the development of two different dance phrases.

Adapted, by permission, from D. Humphrey, 1987, *The art of making dances* (Pennington, NJ: Princeton Book Co.).

Breath Phrasing

The following exploration allows you to practice constructing breath phrases.

1. Practice inhaling and moving a single body part with each breath. Allow your breathing to go into and propel different parts of your body.

2. As you breathe in, allow your breathing to move a single part of your body in any direction you wish. Let this movement continue until you have finished exhaling. On the next breath, begin another breath phrase. Make the length and points of emphasis different in each phrase by playing with both a smooth and an interrupted use of breath.

3. Do the preceding exercise while letting your breath move other parts of your body.

4. Finally, let your breathing move your whole body to form phrases that travel across space. Each phrase should continue for one inhalation and exhalation of breath.

Count Phrasing

Another method of developing a sense of phrasing is to use a certain number of counts for each phrase. For example, you could make the first phrase 10 counts long, the second one 16 counts long, and so on. It might help to have another person clap or beat a drum while you are devising the phrases. The person could even count the number of beats to be included in each phrase so that you're free to concentrate on your movement and its development.

1. Start with a movement in one part of your body, and let it build. Find a conclusion for the developing phrase at the end of 10 counts.
2. Build a second phrase that's longer or shorter than the first one.
3. See if you can link two phrases of unequal length so that as one concludes the other begins. Determine the number of counts to be included in each phrase.

Phrasing of Energy Flow

Energy flow, a third method of developing phrases, requires that you be kinesthetically aware of how you use energy in your body.

1. Begin with an impulse of energy in a single body part, and let it play itself out to an ending. Be sensitive to how you find an ending, or closure, for your movement, and let it develop naturally.
2. Create a series of phrases in that body part by using repeated impulses. When one phrase ends, begin another impulse to start a new phrase.
3. Allow your energy impulses to extend into other parts of your body.
4. Begin to let your energy impulses move your body across space.
5. Vary the quality of energy you use to develop individual phrases. Use sustained, percussive, vibratory, swinging, suspended, or collapsing qualities to create movement.

Phrasing of Set Movements

You can also use set movements to construct movement phrases. It requires you to connect set movements or steps together so that you can perform the entire phrase without stopping between the movements.

1. Practice making a phrase by putting three or four set movements together. For example, a phrase could include two walking steps, four running steps, and a lifting of the arms.
2. Go back over the phrase to analyze how the separate movements connect and how each leads into the next. Decide whether there are adequate transitions between movements.

Music Phrasing

The following explorations should help you construct phrases to music.

1. Listen carefully to a piece of music, and then begin to move. Try to move both on and over the musical beat.
2. As you move, begin to notice where your movements end and how another series of actions begins.
3. Analyze your movement phrasing as it relates to the musical phrasing. Make sure you don't constantly copy the phrasing of the accompaniment.
4. Create several additional phrases with your accompaniment, and include some moments where you hold a pose to provide silences within the phrases.

Characteristics of Effective Choreography

Although there is no single approach to creating a dance that has a clear sense of development, certain characteristics are common to many effective pieces of choreography. Those qualities are unity, continuity, transition, variety, and repetition.

A dance must have **unity.** The separate movements in the choreography must flow together, and each must contribute to the whole; eliminate phrases not essential to the intent of the work. An example of a dance that lacks unity is one in which all movements seem at first to have the same **character** or ambience about them, but then suddenly a movement or series of movements appears that is very different in feeling. Such movements do not fit with the feeling of the choreography; rather, they stand out as distinct from the **essence** of the piece and interfere with the interconnectedness of the dance. It is easier for observers to absorb and get involved in a piece of choreography that maintains unity because it has the capacity to attract and hold the audience's attention.

Continuity is another characteristic of an effective piece of choreography. Choreography with continuity develops in a way that leads to a logical conclusion. The emphasis is on the process of happening, and the observer is swept along to the end. The choreographer provides a natural and organized progression of phrases so that one movement phrase leads naturally into the next.

Transitions from one sequence into another are acceptable because each is an integral part of the choreography and contributes to the unity of the dance. On the other hand, if the observer finds progression from one phrase to another noticeable, the transitions are probably poor. Poor transitions are distracting to the audience because they interfere with **involvement** in the performance of the dance and draw attention to the structure and design of the choreography rather than allow the audience to focus on the overall feeling or form of the work. Transitional movements and phrases help choreography hang together (Schrader 2005).

To maintain the audience's interest, the choreographer must include variety in the development of a dance. The same phrase or movement performed again and again becomes tedious and boring. Contrasts in movement forces and **spatial designs** in the unity of a work add excitement.

Some repetition, however, is important to dance form. Certain phrases need to be repeated in choreography so that the audience can see those movements again and identify with them. Repetition gives a feeling of closure to a work. Repetition emphasizes movements and phrases that are important to the dance; such familiarity with movement is a comfort for the audience (Schrader 2005). Successful repetition of movements usually occurs later in the dance after other phrases have been presented in the intervening time period.

You have probably guessed that a choreographer must maintain a delicate balance between variety, or **contrast,** and repetition. A dance consisting of contrasting movement phrases throughout is just as ineffective as choreography composed of continuously repeated phrases. In the first situation, the audience can't identify with the unrelated string of movements; in the latter instance movements become predictable. Too much variety destroys unity. To help balance variety and repetition, remember that variety is essential to good composition, but it must be used with discrimination.

All the characteristics of effective choreography—unity, continuity, transition, variety, and repetition—are organized to contribute to the development of a meaningful whole. All phrases in a work should be designed to form the integrated sections of your dance, and all the sections of the dance should be placed in a sequence that moves toward an appropriate conclusion. The development of a work should lead the audience logically from the beginning through the middle and on to the end of the dance. The conclusion is the choreographer's own choice; it could be sudden, or it could be gradual so that the dance fades from view.

Observing and Responding

EXPERIENCE IN ACTION

Keep a written record of your discoveries as you go though the following exercises.

1. Watch a videotape of a piece of choreography and decide if the work has a sense of unity and continuity. If you think the choreographer has used those characteristics effectively, point out why you believe it is so.

2. Look at a videotape of the dance and decide if the work contains enough variety. Can you point out or describe some of the actions that provide variety in the choreography?

3. View the videotape with an eye for the way in which the choreographer has included transitions. Does one phrase lead appropriately into the next, or is the sense of the whole disrupted at certain points with movements that do not fit?

4. Notice how the choreographer connects the separate sections of a dance. You might find that use of lighting or music provides a link between sections or that dancers remain onstage to perform transitional movements to connect parts of the dance.

5. As you continue to view the videotape, be aware of repeated movements and movement phrases. Describe how those repeated movements are used throughout the work. In other words, are the movements repeated in the same way, or has the choreographer changed them? Do you find that some movements or phrases are repeated too many times?

6. Discuss your observations with a classmate who has observed the same videotape. Then write your observations in a journal.

Developing Your Skills

VARIETY AND TRANSITIONS

1. One way to include variety is to avoid repeating a movement or phrase in the exact way each time it is included in a work. Try changing the direction, use of energy, or timing of a selected movement.

2. Another method of varying movement is to avoid repeating the movement or phrases on both sides of the body. Constant repetition of a movement right to left or left to right is predictable and uninteresting. Stop and reconsider when you begin to fall into this pattern. Develop a phrase that has one continuous thread of action and that avoids repeating the same movement on the right and then left sides of the body.

3. To practice transitions, find two shapes for your body. Assume the first shape. Move to the second shape by finding a transitional action that carries you to the second shape. Repeat the process several times.

4. Experiment with a variety of transitions between the two shapes in exercise 3 by using both direct and indirect pathways to get from one shape to the others.

5. Choreograph several short movement sequences. Then decide in which stage areas the sequences are to be performed. Finally, choreograph movement transitions that take you from one stage area to the next and that create continuity between the sequences.

Common Choreographic Forms

The overall shape of a piece of choreography can follow many different threads of development. Some of the choreographic forms are unique to dance, but many are based on common musical forms.

AB

The **AB** form is a simple choreographic form that consists of a beginning section, A, followed by a second section, known as B. While sections A and B fit together in terms of the common feeling of a composition, each contains elements that contrast in tone or quality. It could be said that sections A and B share some of the same ground but explore it from different points of view. The choreographer must devise a transition to link the two sections of a dance developed in the AB form. The transition could be presented abruptly or could be produced in a more gradual manner (Blom and Chaplin 1982).

ABA

Another frequently used dance form, **ABA,** has a sense of development that goes a step further than AB. The ABA form is derived from a musical form and has two sections, A and B, followed by an ending A section. In the first part, a series of movement phrases, or theme A, is stated and manipulated. Part B then presents a contrasting theme, and in the final section there is a return to theme A with a twist. A work that follows an ABA format is like life in that it proceeds through the universal pattern of being born, living, and dying (Horst and Russell 1987). All three sections—A, B, and the return to A—fit together to form a unified whole. There should be contrast between parts, yet they should be similar enough to suit the character of the entire dance. Section A, for example, could include large, broad movements, while part B, although choreographed in the same style, might use less space and energy. The third part, the return to A, would be more expansive but with aspects somewhat different from the original A. Again, skillful use of transition is needed between each of the three sections.

Suite

A form of music called the **suite** is also used as a choreographic form. The most typical suite has a moderate beginning, a slow second section, and a fast and lively third section. Many pieces of music written in suite form are excellent accompaniment for dance.

Rondo

The **rondo** is a common dance form. Rondo form repeats musical sections with contrasting sections in between. It can be described as an ABACADAEAFA development of movement ideas. The rondo form consists of an initial section, A, followed by an alternating and contrasting part B. The third section is a return to A, either in its entirety or with some changes. The return to A is followed by a fourth section, C, and another return to A. The remainder of the choreography consists of parts D, E, and F interspersed with variations or restatements of A.

Theme and Variations

Theme and variations is a dance form developed in a manner similar to the musical form with the same name. The choreographer must select a series of movements, called the theme, which is then varied throughout the development of the entire work. The theme can be a single phrase of movements or several movement phrases put together in a sequence. The theme, or original movement series, can be changed in a number of ways as the dance progresses, but the timing and movement sequence of the original theme remain. Changes in a theme could include altering its movement direction or level and giving the movements a different use of quality or dynamics. There should be no repetition of the original form of the whole theme at any point in the dance. The theme and variations dance form is helpful to the choreographer because it provides a limited framework in which movement choices must be made (Humphrey 1987).

Narrative

The **narrative** form of choreography was popular during the early years of modern dance. A narrative composition is sometimes known as a story or **dance drama. Dramatic dances** differ in length and can tell a simple story or communicate a tale of more complex psychological relationships between performers. Narratives choreographed for large groups and those that communicate more complex ideas can last an hour or more, whereas dances choreographed for small groups or for a solo performer may be only minutes long. The narrative choreographic form provides a ready-made framework, since movement choices must relate to the development of the dramatic idea (Humphrey 1987).

Collage

The dance form known as **collage** consists of pieces of movement that are often unrelated but that have been brought together to create a whole. The effect created through this form is at times **surrealistic,** incongruous, comic, or even absurd; it lends itself to dances dealing with insanity or dreams. A collage has movement ideas that may seem disconnected or body parts that may appear disassociated from each other or from actions of the trunk (Humphrey 1987). In a collage it is necessary to have a point of focus in the actions with an overlapping or quick succession of movements (Blom and Chaplin 1982).

Other Choreographic Forms

Although the following additional methods of choreographing can at times provide a formula for a whole dance, these methods usually provide sufficient movement ideas for only a portion of a composition. These forms are tableau, canon, ground bass, and dances devised by chance.

A movement **tableau** is created by having different dancers perform different actions simultaneously in the same space. The effect is one of a large picture or machine that has many moving parts. It would also be possible to choreograph a series of tableaux to create a longer section in a dance. You can do this by placing each tableau at a different location on the stage. Then the dancers would perform transitional movements to connect the tableau sections of the dance. The overall effect would be one of a progression of moving snapshots connected by transitional movements (Minton, submitted for publication). You can also use lighting to highlight the location of each tableau and focus the attention of the audience.

A **canon** consists of one phrase of movement or a longer movement pattern performed at different times by at least two different dancers, although many more performers can be used. In a canon, each dancer executes the entire phrase but starts at a certain number of counts behind another dancer. Each dancer can also begin the phrase at a different point in the series so that one dancer starts on count 2 while another starts on count 6 of the same phrase. In either case, an overlapping visual and temporal effect is achieved, making a canon similar to sequential movement.

The **ground bass** is another choreographic technique. In a ground bass there is a repetition of one movement theme that serves as a background as other themes are brought forward in contrast to the repeated theme (Lockhart and Pease 1982). Usually the repeated theme is performed by a group while a soloist or a smaller group dances the more complex combination of movements. A ground bass can also be performed in a circle; the dancers in the circle would perform the simple, repeated phrase and a soloist or smaller group in the center would perform the contrasting movements. In either type of ground bass, the choreographer exchanges the dancers performing the more complex movements with those in the larger group. This exchange can occur at various times throughout the piece.

Chance, first employed by Merce Cunningham, is another method of manipulating and developing movement. Dance by chance, as mentioned in chapter 2, is a nontraditional choreographic method based on the idea that there is no prescribed order or location for a series of actions. In dances developed by chance, the choreographer gives up some control and allows chance methods to determine the content or organization of the work.

Observing and Responding

EXPERIENCE IN ACTION

1. View a videotape of choreography and determine whether its development parallels the development of one of the choreographic forms described in the previous section.

2. If you can identify the form of the dance, answer the following item that relates to that particular choreographic form.

   - For AB form, identify the contrasting elements in the two sections of the dance, and analyze how the choreographer has created a transition between the sections.

   - For ABA form, identify the contrasting elements in the A and B sections and then determine if the choreographer has used the entire A section, or only a portion of it, in the final part of the dance. Determine how transitions are used between the three sections as well.

   - For rondo, find the separate sections of the choreography and decide how each contrasts with the other. Look for transitions between sections.

   - For theme and variations, discover the movement phrases that make up the theme. Then describe the way in which the choreographer has varied the theme throughout the piece.

   - For a suite, discover where one section ends and another begins. Notice how the tempo changes in the different sections of this dance form.

   - In a narrative, identify the different characters and notice the style of movement used in portraying each personality. Analyze how the choreographer has arranged movement to create a relationship between some of the dancers when a relationship is required in the story.

   - In a collage, discover how the choreographer has achieved a sense of unity among the somewhat-unrelated aspects of the dance. In other words, what is the thread or focus drawing the disparate elements together?

3. View videotapes of other dances that employ the same choreographic form as in exercise 2. Compare the use of the specific dance form in this choreography to the use of the same form in the previous videotape.

4. See if you can find a canon in the dances you have viewed in the exercises. Determine the point at which each dancer begins the repetitive movement of the canon.

5. If any of the videotaped dances demonstrate use of the ground bass, indicate when the ground bass begins and ends. Compare the repetitive actions of the group, the ground, to the more complex movements performed by the figure or figures dancing in front of the group. Point out the transitions used in moving performers between the figure and ground positions.

6. Note your observations in a journal.

Developing Your Skills

CHOREOGRAPHIC FORMS

1. Create an A section by choreographing several phrases of movement. In your B section, come up with several more phrases that contrast but still fit with your first set of phrases.

2. Using the preceding example, a return to a variation of the A section would produce a dance in the ABA form. Create a third section that is a variation of your original A.

3. To create a rondo form from exercise 2, repeat the phrases in section A and then choreograph three or four different sections of movement. These new sections should each be several phrases long. Perform section A followed by a new section, a return to section A, another new section, another return to section A, and so on.

4. In the theme and variations form, the choreographer must vary the same series of phrases. Those phrases are the theme. Come up with a theme and decide how to vary it. You could, for example, change the direction of the thematic movements. Or try moving backward through the sequence instead of forward, use large instead of small actions, or dance with a different quality when performing the separate movements in a sequence. Perform each of the variations by connecting them with transitions.

5. A narrative choreography is based on a story. First decide on the characters and a story, but be clear about how each character fits into the story and relates to the other characters. Then begin to develop movement based on this narrative, but avoid using **pantomime.** You might want to think about a dance with several sections, each of which deals with a specific character or with the relationship between certain characters.

6. In a collage you can use a common thread to link the parts together. The common element could be different colors, varieties of cars, types of flowers, and so on. Using the idea of different colors, come up with movements and phrases that represent each color. Link the phrases together by using transitions between each.

7. Choreograph a series of movements at least 16 to 32 counts in length, and have all of your dancers learn the whole sequence. To create a canon, have the dancers perform the whole sequence with each dancer beginning on a different count. The dancers could begin at evenly spaced intervals two or four counts apart or at unevenly spaced points in the sequence.

8. To create a ground bass, choreograph a simple movement pattern and several sequences involving more detail. Have all the dancers learn the simple movement pattern. (It helps if the simple pattern can be repeated from side to side or in a circle. For example, several walking steps plus a turn constitute a simple pattern.) Teach the more detailed sequences to specific dancers, and then begin by having all the dancers perform the simple, repeated pattern. Next, have one or two dancers move out in front of the group or into the center of the circle to perform the more complex actions. You will need to supply transitions to move dancers out of and back into the group. You should choreograph the transitions so that dancers can reenter the group and immediately begin performing the repeated pattern of the ground.

Relating Form and Content

Movement materials discovered during improvisation are gradually shaped into a dance during the choreographic process. The form should be based on the nature and intent of a composition and should be suitable to the feelings or ideas that you, the choreographer, are trying to present. In the end, you may choose to follow one of the dance forms already described, or you may decide to develop a unique form more appropriate for your choreography. In either case, it is important to perfect your skills so that you have a good sense of development and understand what constitutes a whole dance. Practice in constructing dances based on a prescribed format, such as ABA or theme and variations, is one way to refine your sense of how to shape a dance. When you gain confidence in working with prescribed forms, you can then dare to experiment with developmental ideas that are more personal and uniquely your own. When you have the ability to identify what works choreographically, you are free to mold a dance as you see fit.

To choose an appropriate form for your choreography, you need to identify what you are trying to communicate to the audience. Making such decisions is important to dance making, because when the inspiration determines form, the resulting dance has an organic form instead of being an arbitrary arrangement of movements (Hawkins 1988). The following sections describe several methods of analyzing the inspiration for a dance.

Literal Choreography

In the early years of modern dance it was customary to design dances that told stories. Dances that contain a message, particularly those that communicate a story to the audience, are known as **literal choreography**. Modern dancer Martha Graham created many full-length works that can be described as dance dramas. In these works the performers dance the roles of specific characters and attempt to communicate a story or message to the audience. Two examples of literal choreography in Graham's work are *Appalachian Spring* and *Acrobats of God*. The first of these portrays a young bride and her new husband taking possession of their home and beginning life together on the frontier. In the second work, Graham's intent was to communicate the problems and feelings encountered by a choreographer and the struggle involved in producing creative works (see figures 3.3 and 3.4). In terms of the framework for making dances described in chapter 1, the choreographer observes or gets involved in the characters and story, responds to the story in some way, relates the story to memories and experiences, and uses imagination to transform the response, memories, and experiences into movement and ultimately into a full-blown dance in the literal style.

Nonliteral Choreography

In more recent years the trend has moved away from the literal to create dances in which the choreographer has no desire to tell a story. Such dances are based on design and manipulation; the main concern is experimenting with movement rather than relating a story. A dance deriving its intent from movement design is known as a nonliteral work. **Nonliteral choreography** communicates directly to the audience without explanations; its value is determined by its impact on the perceiver. The viewer cannot find traditional meanings, messages, or morals expressed because nonliteral dances exist simply for the sake of movement. The chance dances created by Cunningham are good examples of nonliteral works. In these dances, Cunningham had no interest in conveying meanings; instead he found his motivation in movement.

Figure 3.3   Martha Graham and Bertram Ross in *Appalachian Spring*.

Figure 3.4   Martha Graham and members of the Graham Company performing *Acrobats of God*.

Choreography Using Abstraction

Some dances are neither literal nor nonliteral. Such works do not tell a specific story, but they do draw inspiration from reality and thus could be considered abstractions from it. These dances draw from life and contain only the essence of the real experience (Hawkins 1988). As an example of a dance that is an abstraction from life, consider one about the sea or the seashore. In such choreography, the dancers' movements would suggest the sea or hint at reactions to the seashore, but there would be no movement included that depicted a pantomime of waves or that portrayed activities traditionally done on a visit to the seashore. Instead, movements would suggest something more general with which most people identify when they think of the sea. A dance that is an abstraction brings forth the essence of the original inspiration. It contains a **semblance** of reality that we can identify but cannot put into words. The framework for making dances described in chapter 1 also applies to the process of abstraction. When working with abstraction, the choreographer observes or gets involved with the inspiration, responds to it in some way, relates the response to memories and experiences, and uses his or her imagination to transform the response, memories, and experiences into movement that represents an essence of the original inspiration.

A sense of form is important to all types of choreography, whether literal, nonliteral, or an abstraction, and whether or not it follows one of the established dance forms described in this chapter. All movements should relate to the intent for creating a work regardless of whether that work is traditional or **experimental.** A sense of wholeness is also necessary. Choreography created with an integral synthesis of parts will be immediately recognized, because such a dance has a life of its own.

Form is not independent, existing as an external container (Blom and Chaplin 1982). Rather, when best used, form grows from content, providing a natural, or organic, dance structure. Organic form, then, is a method of choreographic development that draws on concepts of form that exist in the many patterns and shapes found in nature.

Observing and Responding

EXPERIENCE IN ACTION

1. Watch a video of a piece of choreography and decide if the work fits one of the categories described in the preceding section. Ask yourself whether the piece is literal, nonliteral, or an abstraction.

2. Describe the form and development of the choreography you viewed in the video. Keep a journal of your observations.

3. How would you describe the preceding work if it does not fit into the categories of literal, nonliteral, or abstraction? Record your description of the work in your journal.

4. Does the form used in the latter choreography fit the inspiration? Briefly explain your answer.

5. Would you describe this dance as organic or as having organic form?

6. In your journal, describe how you might have used a different approach to develop the same dance.

Developing Your Skills

USING LITERAL AND ABSTRACTION MODELS

The following improvisations are suggested to clarify the concept of art as literal or as an abstraction from reality. While doing these explorations, remember that abstraction does not mean taking the shape of an inspirational object or pantomiming the typical movements of an animal or person. More sophisticated work in abstraction grows from in-depth movement responses. You can better understand nonliteral choreography by doing the explorations that deal with movement manipulation and variation in chapter 2.

Literal Improvisations

1. Choose a character in a story you have read, and identify the personality traits of that character. In other words, did that person seem to be bright, cheerful, sad, depressed, ruthless, or gentle? Then come up with several movement phrases that you think express the nature of the character.

2. Think about the preceding story again, and decide how the same character changed throughout the book. There were probably some developments in the plot that caused the character to react or take on a different attitude. Choreograph several more phrases that express those changes.

3. Connect the movement phrases that you developed in the preceding two improvisations so that you have a short dance that expresses the changes in reaction and attitude experienced by that character. Try to make your transitions fit the tone and quality of the phrases you have already created.

4. Choose a story that describes a relationship between two people. Improvise movements that suggest the traits of each character. Then decide on how to combine the movements of each to express the relationship between the two. In your journal, write down your movement ideas together with a description of the proposed form and development of the piece.

Abstraction Exercises and Improvisations

1. Play a tape or CD of various sounds that have contrasting qualities. The sounds might include those that are low and calm and others that are high pitched, such as screeching. (This exercise works best with simple, distinct sounds rather than complex music.) As the tape is played, draw on a blank sheet of paper. Create the drawing without much thinking and in response to the quality of the sounds. Relax and use your whole arm to make the drawings. (A felt-tip pen and a fairly large sheet of paper are recommended for this exercise.) If you could compare your drawings to those of another person, you would probably find that a certain kind of sound produced drawings that had a similar quality and shape. This is the essence or abstraction of the inspiring or motivating sound.

2. Listen to each of the preceding sounds again and respond by moving instead of drawing. Movement responses should be based on the quality and shapes you discovered while drawing. Continue to respond to the quality of each sound without thinking about how to move. In this exercise and improvisation, the drawing and then the movement serve as an abstraction of each sound.

3. You can understand abstraction by using visual inspirations as well. Use construction paper in various colors to trigger your movement responses as you improvise.

Although individual responses to specific colors may differ, hot colors such as red usually inspire quick, excited movements, whereas cool colors such as green and blue are met with a more calm reaction. You can respond to the element of shape by cutting the colored construction paper into various shapes.

4. It is easy to connect your understanding of abstraction with the real world. Notice the many sounds, colors, shapes, lines, and designs in your environment, and use them as inspirations to create an abstraction in the form of a short dance.

5. Use your own personal objects as an inspiration for creating abstractions. The objects could include art prints, photos, feathers, plants, and pottery. Begin by selecting the colors, lines, patterns, shapes, and textures found on the objects. Then use these characteristics to inspire your movement.

6. Try using realistic magazine photographs as the motivation for abstracted movement as well.

7. In your journal, record your responses to the preceding exercises and improvisations.

Using Technology to Relate Form and Content

You can use the forms of computer technology discussed in chapter 2 as a link between the form of a dance and its content. For instance, computer-generated images or words projected on a backdrop can enhance and underline the meaning or content of a work. A dance communicates visually through the use of movement direction, shape, size, level, position, and pathway; kinesthetically through the use of energy, rhythm, and timing; and with sound through its accompaniment or dancers' vocalizations. The use of computer-generated images can enhance and refine the intent of a work.

Developing Your Skills

COMPUTER TECHNOLOGY

1. Consider all the dance forms that are described in the section titled Common Choreographic Forms that begins on page 81. Select at least two of the dance forms and describe how you could use computer-generated visual images to enhance dances choreographed in those two forms.

2. How could you use computer-generated words projected on the backdrop to enhance the same two works?

Style of Dance

A final inspiration or intent for creating a dance is to follow a specific movement style. Overall development of a dance based on a specific style can follow some of the forms described earlier in this chapter, or the dance form can be of the choreographer's own design. Common dance styles are jazz, lyric, comic, and geometric. Dance style, in particular, relates to the feeling of a piece, to the way in which energy and rhythm are arranged in a work, and to how the choreographer uses line and shape. It is usually easy to distinguish among various dance styles.

The term *jazz style* is used here to describe traditional jazz dance and its vocabulary of steps as well as original movements and patterns performed in the manner or having the dynamic qualities of traditional jazz. Jazz dance has a syncopated rhythmic pattern similar to that of jazz music. For a jazz-style dance, select movement that is vital and energetic with a captivating energy and rhythm. Jazz-style dancing can be sharp or smooth but frequently involves movements known as **isolations** that are performed with only one part of the body. The rhythms and energy of jazz dance are contagious, and it is difficult to resist the temptation to move when watching such a performance (see figure 3.5). In jazz music the accents are on the weak beats so that in 4/4 time the accents would fall on beats 2 and 4, creating a type of rhythmic variety called syncopation. Jazz music and dance has a pulling, or oppositional, quality.

Figure 3.5   A typical jazz dance movement with bent knee and lowered center of weight.

In contrast to jazz, **lyric** dances are smooth, calm, and controlled. In fact, the movement style in lyric dance is very similar to that of classical ballet, with a rounded use of line and shape. Lyric dancing is traditionally what many people imagine when they think about dance (see figure 3.6).

Figure 3.6   Lyric-style movement. Note the softened, or curved, use of the arms.

Creating dances in a **comic** style requires a special outlook. Comedy does not need to involve the use of complex movement patterns and ideas; rather, it can grow from somewhat simple themes. To compose a comic dance, the choreographer must be able to see the humor in everyday happenings. Comedy relies on an odd placement, or juxtaposing, of the elements of dance design (see figure 3.7).

Figure 3.7 Typical movement from a comic choreography.

Finally, a dance in **geometric** style is one that emphasizes line and shape. The style of dance described here is sometimes called *abstract*, but the word *geometric* is used in this book to avoid confusion with the word *abstraction*, which is choreography based on the essence of something real—a distillation of reality. Geometric dances are nonliteral; the goal is to manipulate movement for the sake of manipulating movement, not to express feeling or intent. When watching a work in geometric style, the observer is drawn into visual designs and impulses and control of energy. The main concern in geometric dance is how the choreographer manipulates these factors in the dance space. Figure 3.8 shows an example of geometric style.

Figure 3.8 Geometric action emphasizing line, shape, and design. (Geometric dance is sometimes known as dance in an abstract style.

As the choreographer, you might decide to compose a literal dance that tells a story or one that is strictly nonliteral. You might even mix some of the dance styles described so that your jazz or lyric composition also communicates a story to the audience. Whatever your motivation in creating choreography, make the dance form you choose fit your inspiration.

Observing and Responding

EXPERIENCE IN ACTION

1. View a videotape of choreography and decide if the work is choreographed in a jazz, lyric, comic, or geometric style. Make a list of the movement characteristics that you believe place the dance in one style category or another.

2. If you concluded that the dance in exercise 1 does not fit any of the style categories defined in this text, decide how you could describe the style of the choreography, and record the analysis in your journal for future reference.

3. View a videotape of a second piece of choreography that you think has a style that contrasts with the style you described in the previous exercise. Compare the style of the first dance with that of the second. In what ways are the two pieces the same? How are they different? Use the elements of movement—space, time, energy, and shape—as the basis for your comparison. In your journal, record the results of your comparison of the styles of the two dances.

Developing Your Skills

STYLE

1. Select a single movement, such as a walk, and perform it in the jazz, lyric, comic, and geometric styles.

2. Do the preceding exploration using other movements. Be aware of the different kinesthetic feelings that accompany the performance of each movement style. Observe your movements in a mirror so that you can see how each style differs visually. Note your observations in your journal.

3. Create a longer sequence of movements—one that is several phrases in length and could be a movement theme in a dance. Then try to perform this theme in each of the four movement styles.

4. Computer-generated images projected on the backdrop can be used for emphasizing the style of a dance. Select two of the dance styles described in the previous section. Then describe the type of visual image you would create and project during dances performed in those styles.

Subject Matter of Dance

The choice of appropriate subject matter greatly affects the development of a successful composition, because form grows from the ideas that inspire your dance. Dance is very ephemeral; the nature of its media—movement—causes it to be so. Movement is seen, and then it is gone. It must be remembered through the images of the mind so that each mental picture adds up in the viewer's memory to form a whole dance that is a complete work of art.

Highly complex subjects are usually inappropriate for choreography. Simple, action-oriented ideas provide much better inspirations for dance compositions because they can be presented and developed more easily. The audience also understands and remembers action-oriented ideas, whereas philosophical ideas can be described more effectively through words or a combination of words and actions. Humphrey (1987) advises that in dance the idea of propaganda or social reform can be overwhelming; cosmic themes such as the creation of the world are too vast; mechanical ideas lead to very mechanical, technique-oriented compositions; and some literary stories can be too complex in terms of the interpersonal relationships involved to be translated into movement, particularly by a beginning choreographer.

Today, through the use of computers and technology, it is possible to clarify complex subject matter in dance. Take the idea of a dance based on propaganda or social reform. When dealing with such a complex subject, the dance itself can communicate the choreographer's reaction to and feelings about the propaganda or social message while images of key personalities or events are simultaneously projected on a screen behind the performers. Key words or phrases could also be used in the projections.

Observing and Responding

EXPERIENCE IN ACTION

1. View several dances on video, and try, if possible, to identify the subject of each without reading a description of the choreographer's intent.

2. In your journal, compare and contrast the form and development used in the dances in the preceding exercise. Write a description of those forms. Notice whether the choreographers have chosen a traditional form such as AB or ABA.

3. Describe the style in which each dance in exercise 1 is choreographed, and record the description in your journal.

4. If a dance you have viewed in the exercise is a nonliteral work, identify what traits or what thread of development hold the work together and give it the sense of being a whole.

Developing Your Skills

SUBJECT MATTER OF DANCE

1. Select a specific feeling, such as happy, sad, or angry. Improvise several phrases of movement that you believe express that feeling.

2. Continuing exercise 1, have a classmate observe your movement phrases to see whether you have been able to communicate the desired feeling.

3. Rework your movement phrases from the previous exercise if you were not successful in communicating the desired feeling. Think about how you could change your use of the elements—space, time, energy, and shape—in order to communicate more successfully.

4. Repeat the improvisation in item 1, but use another inspiration for movement—perhaps one that is movement or action oriented.

5. Select a more complex idea for a dance, and write a description of the development of the choreography.

Finishing touches

Choreographers must learn to look at the total picture that is created in their work. Spatially, dancers form groupings at any single point in time to make ever-changing formations throughout the whole piece. Each of the groupings must be dynamic, not static, creating an interesting and ever-changing series of pictures for the eye so that one part of the dance leads into the next section. Between sections, choreographers should use transitions to give the whole piece continuity and development.

You can begin teaching your movement to your dancers once you have found some phrases through improvisation, have worked with varying those phrases, and have formed an idea for the development of your work. It is possible that the dancers will perform your movements exactly as you visualized, although that is usually not the case. In most circumstances, the choreographer must nurture the execution of the movements by carefully coaching the dancers. The main idea is to make your dance and your performers look as good and as effective as possible.

Communicating With Your Dancers

Projection is one aspect of the dance performance that requires coaching. If a dance is to reach an audience, it must **project.** Dancers must perform with sensitivity and awareness; they must learn to direct energy toward the audience. To aid projection, suggest that your dancers breathe with their movement and allow their energy to flow freely between the center and extremities. In addition, encourage your dancers to reach, stretch, and focus outward while moving.

Choreographers must also communicate with the dancers about the intent of the choreography. Communication can enhance performance quality, enabling performers to get involved in the inspiration for the composition and understand the choreographer's ideas. Appropriate imagery can be a helpful coaching tool here. Try to think of many images that relate to the intent of your choreography, and keep them in mind as you work with your dancers. It might even be helpful to keep a record of **specific images** in your journal that you experienced during the choreographic process. Describe those images to your dancers, particularly when a problem arises concerning the performance of a phrase or sequence. If one image does not connect, try another. Use both visual and kinesthetic imagery. Be persistent and creative in coaching your performers, and don't give up until the execution fits your original inspiration.

As a last resort, if coaching your dancers does not produce the desired result, you may need to simplify or change movements. It will distract from the intent of your work if a dancer cannot perform a movement you have choreographed or if he or she appears tentative when performing an action. Remember, however, that any changes you make in your movements should fit with the intent or style of your dance.

When you've finished setting your work, take time to observe the performance of the dance. A videotape of the presentation can be a useful learning aid at this point. Make a video of the entire choreography, and have the performers watch it immediately. You can point out specific performance problems as the dancers view the tape, but the dancers themselves will notice points at which they have done movements incorrectly. One viewing of a tape usually produces marked improvement in performance quality. Videotapes also provide an excellent method of keeping a record of each of your dances. Store the tapes in a dry, cool place away from heat, light, and electromagnetic sources such as a television, loudspeaker, or microwave oven. Later you should transfer videos of your dances to a computer hard drive, DVD, or CD-ROM so that you'll have a more permanent record of your work.

Developing Your Skills

COMMUNICATING WITH YOUR DANCERS

1. You can learn about projection from the following exploration. Watch a dancer perform a simple action, such as extending the arm diagonally forward from the shoulder. Then have the dancer do the same movement again, this time letting the arm extend as far away from the center of the body as possible. You should notice that the movement appears larger the second time.

2. Another way to enhance projection is to learn to breathe with a movement. In general, dancers inhale as movement progresses up or out, and they exhale as movement comes down or inward. Again, watch a dancer perform a simple action while holding the breath. Then contrast the performance with one in which the dancer does the same movement while breathing. The second performance should appear more full, free, and alive.

3. Use of appropriate imagery can also improve movement performance. Give a dancer a specific movement, and watch as the dancer performs that movement. Then suggest an image that would change and refine the performance of the movement. Experiment with many different images and how each affects the performance of the same movement. (See table 1.1, page 8, for examples of various types of imagery.)

Using Critique and Assessment

As you learn to choreograph, you will put together many dance studies. Your teachers will select appropriate inspirations for those studies and will guide you through the steps of development. Listen carefully to the suggestions about and **assessments** of your work, and relate those suggestions to your developing knowledge of the choreographic craft. Remember that improvement comes gradually and that a critique of your choreography is not a criticism of you as a person. Creating an artistic work can be intensely personal. Try to interpret an evaluation objectively and constructively, not in a negative manner.

The use of a structured assessment form can make a critique more meaningful and objective. Concrete suggestions should make it easier to change and improve your choreography. Assessment sheets can include categories that fit your goals and match the components generally found in a successful piece of choreography. (Appendix B contains a Choreographic Assessment Sheet.) You can fill out an assessment sheet after you have viewed the presentation of your dance. You can write ideas concerning each of the choreographic components on the sheets along with other suggestions for improving the dance. Any ensuing discussion of your choreography then flows from the assessment components, not from purely personal reactions of those who have viewed your dance.

You can also use these or other assessment forms to help you think about your choreography as it develops during the creative process. When you think that specific components need work, make a note of it. Think over possible solutions to the problem, and try to visualize your dancers as they move through each solution. You may need to do more improvisation to solve some choreographic problems.

Through an assessment process, you can take a more positive and active part in the discussion and evaluation of your work. You should find that using assessment forms encourages learning, because you have to understand choreographic components in order to fill out the form.

Observing and Responding

EXPERIENCE IN ACTION

1. Watch a videotape of a dance created by an established choreographer. As you watch, see how the choreographic components discussed in this book were incorporated into the work. Write your observations in a journal.

2. Use the process described in the first exercise to analyze works that you see in live concerts.

3. Watch the same videotape you used in the first exercise, and fill out the Choreographic Assessment Sheet in appendix B.

4. Review the list of choreographic components found in an effective dance (see Characteristics of Effective Choreography, page 79), and then write an explanation of each one using your own words. You will probably discover that your understanding will develop gradually.

Learning Choreographic Form

Hawkins (1988) has said that developing choreographic abilities takes time and occurs in **developmental stages.** It is a trial-and-error process of seeing, experiencing, and learning. Early dances frequently lack clear form and definition. As a novice choreographer, you may find that you create strong beginnings without being able to follow through to a logical conclusion or that you tend to string separate movements together rather than form the movement into sequences or phrases. Viewing the work of established choreographers in live performances or on video is one way to heighten your sensitivity and gain a better understanding of how to mold and give form to your work (see appendix A for a list of videotape distributors). Learning to choreograph is a skill that takes years of practice. The choreographer should learn perseverance, gain worldly experience, and be able to put aside enough time to create and rehearse a dance. An authentic dance composition process, particularly at the beginning level, involves experiencing a struggle to get beyond imitating what other choreographers have done in the past (Lavender 1996).

You will probably be asked to put together many short dances in your choreography class. Each of the short pieces, or studies, usually deals with some aspect of the composition process. In each study, you will work on the forming and shaping process in order to gain a better sense of what makes up a whole dance. Some specific suggestions for exploring and improvising have already been described. The first step in creating either a study or a dance is to discover appropriate movement through exploration and improvisation, as chapter 1 explains. The forming of your dance should follow such experimentation. Your teacher can also provide you with many helpful suggestions concerning choreographic development.

PRACTICAL APPLICATIONS

CREATE

By using the information in this chapter, you should have some idea about how to give form to a dance. To complete the next series of exercises, return to some of the movements, movement sequences, and variations you created in the exercises on pages 70 to 71 in chapter 2. (Those are the movements you created after you studied the sculptures in figure 1.10, *a* and *b*.)

1. Perform the movements and movement variations again, and then decide which set of movements you want to include in your dance—those based on the sculpture in figure 10, *a* or *b*.
2. Next, decide on a tentative, but appropriate, form for your dance.
3. Arrange and rearrange your movements as you progress through the work. Again, think about the ways of arranging your movements that you thought about in chapter 2 with reference to the sculpture.

PERFORM

1. Practice your dance. Then make a video of it and study the video. Determine what seems to work in the dance and what does not work.
2. How does your dance mesh with or compare to your initial inspiration for the piece? In other words, do all of the movements in your dance represent the intent or inspiration for the dance?
3. If some of the movements in your dance seem out of place, do you need to create different movements or rearrange the movements?
4. If you need to create new movements for your dance, what might the new movements look like? If you need to rearrange actions in your dance, how would such a rearrangement of movements look?

REFLECT

1. Once you have made the changes in your dance, perform it again for the video camera. Describe the feelings you experience when you watch yourself perform your dance. Does your dance bring any images to mind or remind you of past experiences?
2. Does your dance convey your feeling response to or ideas about the sculpture in figure 1.10, *a* or *b?*
3. Is the form you used in your dance appropriate, or should your dance follow a different form?
4. Are there any images or ideas that you can focus on to improve the performance of your dance?
5. Imagine the process you used in creating your dance, and describe the steps you used in choreographing this work. Make sure you describe your creative process by beginning with the initial inspiration for the work. Comment on your use of observation, feeling, imagery, memory, and movement transformation during your creative process.
6. Do you think you developed or improved as a choreographer during the process of creating the dance? If so, what aspects or stages of the creative process helped you understand dance making? These were the stages of the creative process described at the beginning of chapter 1.

Choreography Challenge

At the end of chapter 1 in the Choreography Challenge section, you selected an inspiration from the list on pages 5 to 7. Your challenge was to think about your feeling response to the inspiration together with any memories or images that came to mind and then begin to explore and improvise. The next step outlined in the dance-making framework was to vary the movements, create ways to arrange these movements, and begin to form the dance. That step in the framework is the subject of chapter 2. However, as suggested in chapter 1, the dance-making process is circular or spiraling in nature instead of linear. This means that the work with varying and arranging movement in chapter 2 and the work with forming movements into dances in this chapter may be interrupted as you cycle again and again through the entire framework. In this choreography challenge, you will complete the dance begun in the Choreography Challenge sections in chapters 1 and 2 by forming your movements into a dance.

Considering Movement Phrasing

- Review the movements and the movement variations you created in the earlier chapters. Decide whether your movements have a sense of phrasing as described in this chapter.
- Make sure that your movement phrases vary in length.
- Reorganize some of your movement phrases if needed, or create some new ones.

Thinking About Dance Form

- Review the dance forms described in this chapter and choose one of the dance forms that you think is most appropriate for your work.
- The movement phrases you have created may be included at the beginning, middle, or end of your dance. At this point make a decision about which movement phrase will be at the beginning of your piece.

Forming Your Dance

- Perform your first movement phrase and then experiment with the organization of some of the other phrases in your dance. Decide whether you need to create movement transitions between the phrases. Create more variations of your movement phrases if needed.
- Set your work on your dancers using the form you selected, but be open to making changes if needed.
- Return to the studio and rework movements or create new movements when problems arise.
- Return to rehearse with your dancers again and again, making necessary changes. Keep the criteria of good dance form in mind as you work back and forth between your creative process and the rehearsals with your dancers.

4

Staging
the Performance

Planning a dance performance can be a daunting task, but you can minimize the challenge by arranging the production process into a series of smaller, more digestible tasks. You can schedule each of the individual tasks by beginning with the date of the performance and working backward to the audition. This chapter deals with getting your dance ready for performance. In terms of the framework presented in chapter 1, the information presented here is to be used after you have finished creating your work.

At one point, I choreographed and designed the costumes for a five-part dance based on Mayan artifacts and mythology. In many ways I attribute my ability to complete that project to the fact that I had planned when the choreography, costume designs, and costume and mask construction needed to be completed. By organizing my schedule, I was able to treat each task as one step in producing a large creative work.

A successful dance concert is well organized. This means that you have considered all aspects of production from the audition to the closing performance. This chapter begins with an introduction to the audition and the process of scheduling rehearsals. Blocking, technical rehearsals, and dress rehearsals are discussed, followed by information about dance floors and the printed program. As the technical aspects of a dance concert can enhance or detract from the production, you'll find many suggestions about how to record the accompaniment, design the costumes and lighting, and use props and sets. At the end of this chapter, you will also learn how to stage informal concerts and lecture-demonstrations.

Planning and Organization

You should plan the content of a performance carefully, whether the concert is formal or informal. Program content should be based on the interests and needs of both the dance students and the audience. You won't build an audience unless you attempt to connect with the needs and ideas of potential audience members. For example, it wouldn't be wise to produce an experimental dance concert in a conservative community. Similarly, dance concerts presented in neighborhoods made up of people of a certain ethnic group should include some representation of the dance forms derived from the predominant culture. If you're living in a community where dance is not understood, you may need to do some audience education. The information that informs the audience about dance usually takes the form of program notes, program inserts, or a lecture-demonstration. (The lecture-demonstration is discussed later in this chapter.) A community that is knowledgeable about dance will be able to appreciate a dance concert without the aid of explanations, but program content should still be planned to suit community tastes.

You should also consider program variety when planning a concert—particularly with respect to choreographic styles and the number of performers in each dance. Try to alternate the order of light and serious compositions and of small and large groups. Other suggestions are placing an entertaining but short dance first to allow late arrivals to be seated fairly quickly, presenting another entertaining dance immediately before intermission to make the audience want to come back for the second part of your show, and saving the best for last so the concert builds in energy and impact toward the end. Program order should be based on practical considerations as well. For instance, it may be necessary to have some quick costume changes when the same dancer or dancers perform in one piece right after another. Try to accomplish the costume changes rapidly and smoothly, but if you are able to arrange your concert to avoid quick changes, do so.

Holding Auditions

The audition—the first step in producing a dance concert—is a process that has made many dancers nervous. Learning new movement materials, performing in an unfamiliar space, and dancing in front of strangers can all contribute to a case of nerves. Encourage dancers to arrive at your audition early. This will give them time to warm up and also allow them to relax, select a dance space, and get a feeling for the space in which the audition will be conducted.

You can do many other things as well to make auditioning less hectic and better organized. One idea is to have each dancer fill out an information sheet and assign him or her a number (see appendix B for a sample Dancer's Audition Form). Two of the most important pieces of information for you on the sheet are the phone number and the times when the dancer is available for rehearsals. Have dancers attach their numbers to their dance clothing so that you'll be able to identify each dancer by number if you do not know the person's name. This is important because dancers are often cast during a meeting that follows the audition session. Dancers should audition in the same numerical order throughout the entire session.

Begin the audition by teaching your movement patterns to the whole group. Each movement sequence you present should be representative of the type and style of movement found in the choreography. In addition, choose movement sequences that are relatively short and simple in order to keep audition time to a minimum. The dancers will need time to practice each sequence and to ask questions if necessary. Finally, you can watch while the dancers perform the sequence. This performance should be done in small groups so that you'll be able to see each dancer. You can watch the first 10 dancers, then the next 10, and so on. You'll need to repeat this process for additional dances to be included in the concert. Select the dancers who perform your movements with a sense of clarity, accuracy, understanding, and vitality—they will contribute most to the success of your work. You should also choose dancers who pick up your movements quickly, perform your choreography in the appropriate style, project well, seem cooperative, respond to suggestions, and pay attention during the entire audition process.

If you're composing more than one dance, try to distribute the performers among the choreographic works so that no one dancer is in an excessive number of dances and so that all or most dancers will get some performing experience. The cast list should be posted as soon as possible—preferably the morning after the audition. Dancers should read the list and put a check after their names so that you will know they have read the cast list. It's also helpful to include on the cast list the date and location of the first rehearsal of your dance.

Developing Your Skills

HOLDING AUDITIONS

For this series of exercises, use the dance you created in the Choreography Challenge at the end of chapter 3.

1. Design a sample audition information sheet, making sure the sheet includes space for all necessary information.

2. Prepare the dancers' numbers on small squares of paper. The papers should be sized so that they do not interfere with dancers' movements, but the numbers should be large enough to be seen from your vantage point at the front of the

room. You'll need small safety pins for attaching the numbers to each dancer's clothing. Do not use straight pins for this purpose.

3. Visualize how you want the dancers positioned in the audition space. For example, in which direction should they face and on which pathways will they move across the floor? Decide on how many dancers you want to view in each group.

4. Select the movement sequences you will use in auditioning dancers for each work. Practice each sequence with everyone who is auditioning. Supply other movement cues to enhance understanding of the performance of the pattern. Use images or ideas that describe the desired movement qualities in the sequence.

Scheduling Rehearsals

A well-organized rehearsal schedule is essential for a successful performance. Try to schedule two or more rehearsals each week. The rehearsals should be long enough to allow sufficient progress but not so long that the dancers become exhausted. You will have many rehearsals before your dance is moved into the theater. One thing you can do to make the transition from studio to theater easier is to tape the stage dimensions on the dance studio floor. It's also helpful to mark dancers' beginning or ending positions and the placement of sets.

Blocking Rehearsals

You should schedule theater rehearsals by beginning with the performance and moving backward to the date on which you first have use of the theater. The first theater rehearsal is for blocking. Usually there will be time for only one blocking rehearsal, which is used to **mount** the dance on the stage. You should try to leave more time to block a long dance, but bear in mind that the blocking time will depend on the total time you are allowed in the theater.

Begin blocking rehearsals by having the dancers run through the entire piece. As you do this, decide where you need to reposition dancers. Next, go through the choreography slowly, and direct the placement of each dancer; be clear about the floor patterns that each dancer is to follow throughout the progression of the piece. You should also indicate how performers are to relate to each other in the stage space and where each dancer enters and exits. As a safety precaution, clarify the position of all onstage technical equipment. The dancers must know the placement of all **masking,** wiring, lighting, and sound equipment so that there are no dangerous surprises during the program! All loose wires should be taped down, and pieces of carpet should be placed over sharp or protruding equipment to prevent injury during entrances and exits. This is also the time to warn dancers about **sight lines,** since performers should not be visible until they are part of the action onstage. A good rule is to have your dancers stand very close to and behind the **leg** (side curtain) when awaiting an entrance. Generally, if dancers can see members of the audience from where they are standing, then those audience members can probably see the dancers as well.

In some concerts you might be able to close the front curtain after each dance, but in theaters in which that is too time consuming, it is advisable to have dancers enter the darkened stage with the front curtain open. In the course of an entire performance, then, the curtain would be closed before the concert, at intermission, and after the last dance. If the curtain remains open between dances, entrances should be made in a calm and collected manner; also, dancers will find their starting positions more easily if the stage floor is marked with fluorescent tape.

It is customary to have the performers take a bow after a dance. The bow puts a professional and finishing touch on the choreography. After the dance is ended, the performers come back onstage as quickly as possible, the lights are brought back up, the dancers bow, the lights go down, and the dancers exit. In most bows, the performers stand in one line and bend forward from the waist; the dancer on the far right or left leads the line. A large bow with a flourish of movement down to the floor is considered in bad taste. Taking a bow two, three, or more times in succession; making various facial expressions such as grinning, nodding, or winking at the audience; or having each dancer bow in a different way or at a different level detracts from the performance too. Waving, pointing, or gesturing at friends and family members in the audience is also in poor taste. On the other hand, a bow in which the performers assume a pose from the choreography rather than take a traditional bow can be effective (see figure 4.1, *a* through *c*). You should have your dancers practice the bow during the blocking rehearsal. Be sure to include a bow for the accompanists if your work is performed to live music.

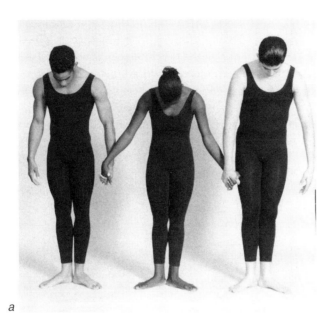

a

b

c

Figure 4.1   *(a)* A simple bow with clean lines; *(b)* a bow that is too distracting; *(c)* a choreographed pose instead of a traditional bow at the conclusion of a dance.

Technical Rehearsals

Technical rehearsals usually follow blocking rehearsals. In technical rehearsals, the technicians have a chance to set and practice lighting cues, and the performers in turn become familiar with those cues. Technicians, particularly those who are not familiar with dance, may need to see a movement several times before they are able to connect it with the appropriate lighting cue. For this reason, it is helpful to have the **lighting designer** attend rehearsals before the concert is moved into the theater.

In the technical rehearsal, have the performers mark through the entire piece of choreography, stopping at each point at which a change should occur in the lighting. Sometimes lighting cues can be coordinated with counts in accompaniment, but for most dance performances, particularly modern dance concerts, lighting cues should be keyed to dance movements or poses. This is also the time to experiment with the use of various **gel** colors and with instruments located in various positions. (See the section titled Color Gels, page 119, for an explanation of how to use gels.) The lighting designer must write down each cue, indicating which instruments (such as spotlights, striplights, or floodlights) are needed for producing the desired effect. All cues must be numbered from the beginning to the end of the concert and should note how a particular cue can be used for enhancing the choreography and how it relates to specific changes in the dance. Cues should also include information about how to control lighting changes at the **dimmer** board and, if necessary, the duration of the cue. Never recommend that cues be memorized; the large number of cues required during a dance performance makes memorization extremely difficult.

You or your technicians may have to rerun certain segments of a dance several times until the lighting is done correctly. Later, you will practice each lighting cue again as the dance is performed during the dress rehearsals. If you have time during the technical rehearsal, run the dance together with the lighting cues immediately after the cues are set. Try to allow a long block of time for the technical rehearsal of your dance, since you'll usually have only one session in which to set the cues.

Dress Rehearsals

Dress rehearsals are conducted before the actual concert and should be run more than once if time in the theater permits. During dress rehearsals, you have a chance to give lighting and costumes a final check. This is also when the pace of the entire program can be brought up to speed. Remember that audiences get restless at dance concerts that have long breaks between each piece. Dancers should be encouraged to make entrances and exits as quickly and smoothly as possible; performers who dance in two or more consecutive dances should practice changing costumes. Sometimes you can accelerate the flow of a concert by providing **dressers** to help with quick changes. A dresser has a costume ready and helps undress and dress a performer; a small portable dressing room can be set up behind a screen in the **wings** to facilitate quick costume changes. All rehearsals, including the choreographer's rehearsals, should be written on a calendar and posted where the entire cast can check the schedule (see appendix B for a sample Performance Organization Checklist to help you organize audition and rehearsal scheduling).

Developing Your Skills

PLANNING REHEARSALS

Use a block calendar to organize the following schedule. The block calendar will be your **master calendar.**

1. Begin with the date of your performance to determine when you should hold the audition for your dance. (This block of time may already be determined by your department or school.) The audition date should immediately precede the onset

of rehearsals so that you have several months in which to create your dance. However, if you're given less time in which to rehearse, organize your rehearsal schedule accordingly. Be practical, but try not to sacrifice the quality of your dance.

2. Next, schedule your weekly rehearsals. At least two rehearsals per week are recommended in order to provide continuity and to help your dancers remember the choreography. Check the audition forms for the best rehearsal time for each dancer, and post the rehearsal schedule after the audition.

3. Mark off the time in which you will be allowed to rehearse in the theater. Then divide this allotment of time into the blocking, technical, and dress rehearsal.

   - Blocking a choreographed piece usually requires one to two hours, but it can take less time for a short dance.

   - Technical rehearsals usually require more time. A long dance with many cues could take an entire evening, since the technical rehearsal involves experimenting with the lighting and writing down the cues.

   - Dress rehearsals should take place immediately before the performance. Again, the number of dress rehearsals is determined by the total amount of time you have in the theater. It is ideal to have three dress rehearsals, but sometimes that might not be possible. Use full makeup only in the final dress rehearsal.

4. If you can, leave some theater rehearsal time for changing the lighting, for holding additional rehearsals if there are problems, and for taking record photographs. Mark all these events on your master calendar.

5. Use the Performance Organization Checklist in appendix B to help you organize a rehearsal schedule. Put a check in front of each item as you include it in your schedule; then record on your master calendar the dates on which you plan to conduct each type of rehearsal.

6. Briefly explain your organization of the master calendar, telling how this arrangement fits your situation. For example, why were the blocking or technical rehearsals arranged as represented?

A Word About Dance Floors

The ideal dance surface is a **suspended floor** that is smooth, unblemished, and free of splinters. Theaters that have cement stage floors are not appropriate for dance and should be avoided if possible. Carefully check the surface of your stage floor. Look for nails, screws, or other sharp objects that could injure dancers' feet. Cover splintered areas in the floor with masking tape, and then paint the tape the same color as the floor so it will not be noticed. Clean the stage floor with a damp mop before each rehearsal and performance to remove dust that could soil costumes. For future reference, a listing of some of the companies that sell portable **dance floors,** along with additional information about the floors, is provided in appendix A.

Developing Your Skills

CHECKING THE DANCE SURFACE

1. Find a space in which you could present your dance. This should be a stage or studio space to which you have access. Walk slowly back and forth across the space, inspecting the surface of the floor for splits, splinters, or small objects that could injure your dancers or interfere with their performance. Decide where you might put tape to cover rough areas or holes.

2. Determine whether the surface of the floor needs to be mopped.

3. Inspect the areas located on the edge of the performance space. Make sure that no chairs, ladders, or other pieces of equipment block the dancers' ability to make entrances and exits. If such equipment is in the way and cannot be moved, decide how you could alter your choreography so that the obstructions are no longer a problem.

4. Mark your master calendar to indicate an appropriate time in which you could conduct the inspection of the performance space. The inspection should take place before blocking rehearsals begin.

Printed Program

The printed program should give credit to all the individuals involved with the creation of your dance, since only the performers are seen onstage. Program notes can also help the audience understand and appreciate your work, and if your dance is performed in more than one location, it can serve as a map.

The printed program should include the following information:

- Title of dance
- Grants and funding sources
- Choreographer
- Musical artists and composers
- Title of music
- Recording company label
- Credits (costume designer, props construction, lighting designer, and so on)
- Dancers (in alphabetical order)
- Program notes
- Other information such as the technical director, dance concert director, stage manager, master electrician, sound and light board operators, and house manager (usually listed following the listing of all the dances)

The title of a dance is a guidepost for the audience. Choreographers should use dance titles that hint at the nature or content of the dance. This sets the stage and points the way, indicating in general what is to come and what the audience can expect from a choreographed piece. At the same time, a title should leave some of the mystery about a dance intact, allowing members of the audience to explore their imagination concerning the work and to experience the choreography on their own terms.

Good names for dances are often suggested by the title or style of the accompaniment, the style of the choreography, or a relationship created between the performers. Dance dramas can bear names that hint at the story told in the dance or that relate to some of the major characters. Both the dance title and the program notes should grow from the motivating materials with which you have been working rather than serve merely to describe the action of the dance. Titles for nonliteral dances are used as a **metaphor** or clue to help spectators get involved in the choreography and provide a reference point or place to begin viewing the work (Turner 1971). Often such titles are based on choreographic concepts such as imagery, movement quality, and dance form (see table 4.1 for an analysis of dance title and content).

On program copy, the dancers' names are usually listed in alphabetical order, although you may also list performers in the order of their appearance in your dance. Sometimes the major dancers and the roles they perform are grouped separately. For legal or copyright protection, list the label on the tape or compact disc so that the music publisher receives credit

Table 4.1 Dance Titles and Content

Dance title	Dance content
Legends of the Maya	A five-part piece dealing with Mayan legends. These legends include stories of Mayan gods and the Mayan creation myth.
Under-Currents	A dance in which the three sections portray the themes of searching, aggression, and harmony.
Electronic Terpsichore	A three-part dance choreographed to a whimsical, electronic score.
Ritual Dance	A two-part dance based on the movement themes of tribal peoples.
Three Episodes	A three-part lyric dance in which each part has a theme or thematic element. For example, in part I, the dancers attempt to upstage each other, and in part III small balls are exchanged among the dancers.
Kinetic Rhythm	A fast-paced jazz-style choreography.

in the program. Under credits, list the names of others who have made contributions to your work, such as costume designers, technical designers, props people, and visual artists. If you received a grant or donation to produce your work, make sure to note that source in the program; consult a representative of the benefactor or foundation to make sure the organization is credited correctly. You may need program notes to explain characters or meanings in your dance; if so, try to keep the notes clear and brief. Some programs also list a rehearsal director if there is one. Dance concerts that are collaborative performances presented by various groups or companies should include some information about each group. Provide the name of the contact person, an address, a phone number, and some background information about the group. This information helps publicize these groups. Appendix B includes both a sample Printed Program Information Sheet (used for collecting and organizing information for the printed program) and a sample program entry.

Developing Your Skills

CREATING THE PRINTED PROGRAM

1. Create a title for your dance by reviewing the information in the preceding section. Remember this is the dance you completed in the Choreographic Challenge at the end of chapter 3. A few potential titles may have occurred to you during the creative process, and you may still think that one of those titles is the right one. (It's a good idea to make note of all potential titles as they come to mind and record them in your journal.)

2. Explain your choice of title for your choreography.

3. Use the Printed Program Information Sheet in appendix B to compose other information concerning your dance that will appear in the printed program.

4. Format the program entry for your dance, and produce a printed copy for your records.

5. Return to your master calendar and select the dates for creating and printing program copy.

Technical Considerations

A considerable amount of finishing needs to be done even after a dance is choreographed and the movement is set on the dancers. Some of this polishing is accomplished by coaching the dancers, but presentation of the final product requires that the director go through several other steps:

- Recording the music
- Designing and executing the costumes
- Planning the lighting
- Creating sets and props
- Assigning props to a prop master
- Working with a computer person to design images and other effects that require the use of technology
- Working with theater technicians to coordinate the operation of computer-generated images and effects

Organizing the rehearsal schedule—including blocking, technical, and dress rehearsals—is also part of the final stages of performance production.

Preparing the Accompaniment

Dance accompaniment is best when performed live. This is true of both classroom accompaniment and accompaniment for dance performances. However, while live accompaniment provides better quality and greater flexibility than recorded sound, the cost of paying musicians is usually beyond the budget of most choreographers.

If recorded accompaniment is used, it must be of high quality. The director or sound person should use new tapes, discs, or records for the **master tape,** disc, or sound files. Old recordings are likely to produce a sound track with many pops and cracks, and those extraneous sounds are magnified when reproduced over a loudspeaker system. When making recordings, keep the volume at a uniform but high level, since the use of different audio levels requires constant adjustments in volume during the performance. Use cables and plugs to produce recordings, because microphones allow extraneous sounds to be picked up by recording equipment. Do not cut music or change the speed of the original score.

If possible, use the most recent developments in computer technology to provide accompaniment for your concert by digitally saving music files to a computer program or MP3 player. Such programs can be shown on the computer screen; as the music is played, a bar moves through a visual time line to indicate the beginning, middle, or end of the accompaniment. Markers can also be added to remind the technician about cues during the performance.

There is also the possibility of recording your accompaniment on a CD. Although a CD produces a higher-quality sound than a tape, it cannot be labeled for cueing purposes. The MiniDisc, produced by Sony, is a recent development in CD technology that allows you to record your own music and insert marker points for cues. Recording your accompaniment on a MiniDisc will allow the technician to locate music by keying in a specific track. In addition, digital audiotapes are quickly taking the place of the other types of audiotapes. A digital tape operates on the same principle as your computer because the input is transformed into numbers; thus when sounds get louder, the numbers get larger. Digital audiotapes look like other types of audiocassettes but are smaller, produce a higher-quality sound with no hiss, and can be electronically marked with cues for start and stop points.

If you use a tape player during your performance, make sure that the format used for recording matches the format of the playback unit so that both units are either **stereo** (involving the use of separated microphones and two transmission channels to achieve the sound separation of live hearing) or **monaural** (involving a single transmission path). Audiocassettes can be used for the master tape, but it is more difficult to locate specific points on a cassette than on a reel-to-reel tape. Use of a reel-to-reel tape recorder allows the sound person to view the tape during the performance in order to locate specific points on the tape more easily (see figure 4.2). When recording master tapes, splice a light-colored leader between each musical selection. This will allow you or your audio technician to see where you've stopped the tape and also to stop only at a point between the accompaniment for specific dances. It's a good idea to write the name of each piece of choreography on the leader preceding the accompaniment to prevent mistakes in pausing the tape during a concert. Labeling each piece also enables you to cope with last-minute problems, such as the need to delete a dance from the program. So you'll be prepared in case of emergency, make a copy of your master tape, and have it available

Figure 4.2   A reel-to-reel tape re-corder.

during all performances. If you are using a cassette player for your performance, you should have the music for each dance recorded on a separate cassette. In this way, you could still alter the order of the concert or remove a dance if necessary. Label each tape clearly, and do not record on the back side of any of the cassettes. Extra computers, other types of playback equipment, CD players, or tape recorders should also be on hand for a show so that you can easily deal with emergencies.

The audio technician should attend some of the early rehearsals to learn the sequence of movements that make up each composition and to take notes concerning each cue or change in accompaniment. Sound cues include changing volume, fading sound in and out, and turning accompaniment on and off.

Check the speakers to be used during the performance. If they produce poor-quality sound, replace them with better equipment. When possible, use a stereo rather than a monaural sound system, and always check sound quality from different areas in the house. It is sometimes necessary to place a portable speaker on each side of the stage to provide adequate sound for the performers. If you do this, make sure sounds don't bleed into the theater by placing the speakers downstage and directing them on upstage diagonals rather than directing speakers out toward the audience or straight across the stage from right to left. It's also a good idea to place microphones onstage to amplify the voices of speaking dancers or to pick up foot sounds such as taps.

Developing Your Skills

PREPARING THE ACCOMPANIMENT

1. Listen carefully to the downloaded music, CD, or tape track that you have chosen for your accompaniment. Notice if there are extraneous sounds.

2. If you can hear extraneous sounds in your music, get a new copy of it if possible.

3. Record your accompaniment using good equipment. You may need a skilled technician for this purpose.

4. Listen to your recorded music, and repeat the recording process if necessary.

5. Before dress rehearsals, test the master of the recorded accompaniment to be used during the performance. This step is important, since your dancers may need to accommodate a slight change in tempo. The speed at which tape recorders, in particular, reproduce sound can differ, even though each recorder is put on an identical setting. Find other equipment if the difference in tempo is excessive.

6. Mark your master calendar to indicate recording dates.

Costuming the Dance

One of the first rules of dance costuming is to make sure the costumes complement the choreography, not detract from it. A dance costume should enhance the movement. The most effective costumes, therefore, are simple in design. You have defeated your purpose if the audience focuses on costumes rather than the dancing. You should begin to visualize costuming as soon as you have a movement sketch or basic outline of your choreography.

The costumes for a dance should be developed from the same ideas that inspired the creation of the choreography. As you consider costume design, review the feeling, intent, or style that you are trying to create in your piece. Clarify this intent and keep it in mind while you decide on appropriate costumes. Then make some sketches of the proposed costumes. Remember that costumes help create mood. Notice that in figure 4.3 the costumes are playful and comical, whereas in figure 4.4 the costumes project a more serious mood. The costumes in figure 4.5 place the dance in a specific historical period. Also consider the following features with respect to dance costumes:

Figure 4.3 Leotards and tights put together with colored wigs and leg warmers create a simple but comical costume.

Figure 4.4 Here unitards provide costumes for a more serious dance.

Figure 4.5 A costume from a period in American history. Doris Humphrey (center) in her choreography *The Shakers*.

- Colors
- Flow and weight of materials
- Style and decoration

Color

Costume color plays a major role in setting the feeling of a piece. Colors such as red, yellow, brown, orange, pink, and rose are considered warm. Green, blue, gray, purple, lavender, and black are cool. You must also think about your dancers when selecting costumes and take into account their coloring, body build, and respective heights. Choose costume colors that are complementary to your dancers' coloring, and remember that dancers appear more slender when clothed in darker colors. Lighter-colored or more brightly colored costumes should be worn by dancers with trim bodies. If it is necessary to costume a less trim dancer in a light- or brightly colored costume, select costumes that camouflage wide hips or other imperfections. You can do so by adding stripes or patches of a darker color in strategic places on a costume (see figure 4.6). Bear in mind that white costumes tend to produce a glare under stage lighting, although the glare can be reduced by dipping the costumes into tea. This process will produce a more subdued shade of off-white that will reflect less light.

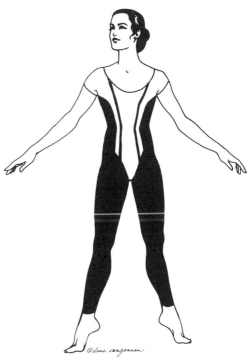

Figure 4.6 Vertical panels and stripes have a slimming effect.

Sometimes the choreographer or costume person will have to dye costumes that are white. Dyeing costumes a light shade is usually more successful than trying to create vibrant or deep shades; if you desire costumes in deep shades of a color, you should purchase them. It is also difficult to dye one part of a costume to match another part.

The texture and type of material affect the way a costume will accept a dye. In general, synthetic materials do not accept dye as well as organic fibers such as cotton. When in doubt, test a swatch of the material in the dye before immersing the entire costume. Attempts to remove color from a costume and dye it another hue are usually not successful—a rather gray shade of the desired color results and can be difficult to correct.

A choreographer can use costuming to enhance the overall effect of a grouping of dancers, even though individual dancers are of various heights and body structures. Dressing all dancers in one color creates unity, although you can create a more interesting effect by using more than one shade of the same color within a group (see figure 4.7a). In this way, unity is maintained, but the stage space appears to have greater depth and more interest. On the other hand, if you place each performer in a different color or in a different-style garment, harmony is lost because the audience focuses separately on each dancer (see figure 4.7b). If possible, the soloist should be costumed in a style or color somewhat different from those worn by other performers (see figure 4.7c). Avoid the use of large and bold prints, plaids, and stripes because they tend to distract the audience from the dance.

a

b

c

Figure 4.7 *(a)* Group unity and design are heightened through use of the same-color costumes. *(b)* Audiences tend to focus individually on each dancer in a group when they are costumed differently. *(c)* The use of a different color calls attention to the downstage dancer.

Flow and Weight of Materials

You can select materials for dance costumes from a fabric store. When you find a material in the right color, unwind some of it from the bolt and move it around to see how it flows.

Stiff materials, for example, will stand away from the body and hide and inhibit a dancer's movements. Instead, select fabrics that will flow with a performer's actions. If possible, test a material by draping some of it on one of your dancers and watch the dancer move in the material. Also consider the weight of the fabric. Very lightweight fabrics, such as nylon chiffon, create a floating effect when a performer moves, whereas fabrics that have more body, such as jersey, flow with the dancer but tend to cling even as the dancer moves.

Unoccupied spaces around the body (negative spaces) are frequently part of the dance design and should not be covered or filled in with material. Long skirts, for example, can fill in negative spaces. In addition, certain textures are more appropriate for some types of costumes than for others. For example, roughly textured materials should be used to clothe dancers portraying lower-class characters, while plush materials are reserved for royalty. Shiny materials reflect light and should be employed sparingly; reflected light attracts attention and should be used only for that purpose.

A costume can also help to extend and vary movement. A long, flowing skirt heightens the effect of actions performed with the legs; the choreographer can even use such a skirt to help find movements during the improvisation process. A flowing cape, long sleeves, headgear, or fabrics that stretch can enhance dance movement and become part of the choreographic design as well. (Refer again to figures 4.4 to 4.6.)

Style and Decoration

A basic leotard is the best costume for most student performances. It is a good idea to build up a stock of plain leotards in many different colors. They can then be paired with tights of the same or a contrasting color for use in different concerts. Leotards in unusual colors or of an unusual design cannot be adapted as readily for use in later performances.

Give careful consideration to the style and cut of your costumes. Figure 4.8, *a* through *c* illustrates examples of poorly designed dance costumes. In figure 4.8a, the costume is too intricate and would divert attention from the choreography. That costume would also inhibit movement by getting in the way. The garment shown in figure 4.8b cuts the body horizontally, making the dancer appear short and stocky rather than tall and lean. Figure 4.8c shows

Figure 4.8   *(a)* Highly detailed and intricate costumes distract from the movement. *(b)* A costume with horizontal panels or stripes would not be appropriate for a short, stocky dancer. *(c)* This leotard could not be adapted easily for use in later performances.

a leotard that cannot be adapted for use in many separate concerts because the design is not easily used in combination with other costume pieces or decorations.

The **unitard,** or body suit, is a popular dance costume. Unitards are made in one piece to cover the entire body. Decorations can be added, and they are available in styles with or without sleeves and with various necklines. Unitards are made of an elasticized material that fits the body closely and thus are not flattering to some dancers. A unitard costs about the same as a pair of tights and a leotard together, but it is not as versatile. (See figure 4.9.)

Choreographers can add various decorations to unitards and leotards, but decorations should be used sparingly and should fit the overall design concept. Decorative costume pieces could include collars, necklaces, armbands, leg bands, belts, and sleeves—all of which can be made more durable by applying an iron-on fabric stiffener. Costume parts can be held to the underlying garment with hooks or snaps, but small pieces of Velcro fabric are recommended as fasteners for quick changes because they are easy to pull apart and press together. Velcro strips can be

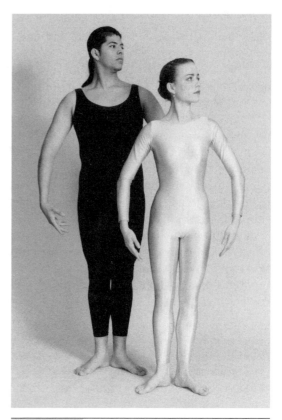

Figure 4.9   These dancers are wearing unitards.

purchased in most fabric stores in sew-on and iron-on forms. Make sure, however, that the ripping sound made by separating large Velcro strips cannot be heard by the audience and that such fasteners are positioned so as not to come loose during partnering work. Test all costume parts during the dress rehearsals.

You can also change the look of plain unitards and leotards by having dancers wear skirts, pants, or various kinds of tops over the undergarment. You might want to experiment with dyed or painted decorations as well. Dye can be spattered, sprayed, or dusted (in dry form) onto a costume to create abstract designs. You can also use a batik process to create designs on costumes. In this process, fabric is hand-dyed after wax has been applied to specific areas to act as a dye repellent. However, you should use paint to create more precise images. Acrylic and latex paints work well on fabrics because the fabric remains flexible and can be laundered.

Observing and Responding

EXPERIENCE IN ACTION

1. Watch a video of a performance by a well-known dance company. Select one dance on the video and note how the choreographer has used costuming to enhance the style or mood of the work.

2. Make a descriptive list of the choreographer's use of color, material, costume style, and decoration throughout the dance chosen in exercise 1. Then explain how each costume element complements the structure, mood, or message of the

choreography. If you find the use of some elements of the costuming unflattering or distracting, explain.

3. Look at a video of a second dance and analyze the choreographer's use of costumes in the same way as in the preceding exercise. Compare and contrast the costume choices made for each piece. Why do the costumes differ in the two works?

4. Record your observations and thoughts in your journal. What ideas does watching this performance give you for your own choreography?

Developing Your Skills

ENVISIONING THE COSTUME

1. Review the mood or style of your choreography. Try to picture the basic color that you believe complements the mood.

2. Browse through a fabric store. When you find material in an appropriate color, unwind some of it from the bolt and test it for movement quality.

3. Buy a small piece of material of the "right" color and movement quality. The piece should be large enough to cover part of a dancer's body. Drape the material on one of your dancers, and watch how it moves as the dancer performs your choreography.

4. Visualize various costume possibilities that might be suitable for your choreography, and sketch those costumes on an outline of the human figure. (Trace the human figure from a book or magazine if your drawing skills leave something to be desired.) As you sketch costume possibilities, be aware of the cut and flow of the garments. Use felt-tip pens to color your drawings, and then add possible designs or decorations using the same-color or different-color pens.

5. Select one of your designs from the preceding exercise for your dance, and explain why you selected that costume. Record some of your costume ideas and descriptions in your journal.

6. Mark your master calendar to indicate dates for completing costume designs and construction.

Lighting the Dance

You should keep two main concepts in mind when you're planning the lighting of a dance: stage space and lighting direction. It is also important to understand the controllable qualities of light: intensity (brightness), distribution, movement, and color. The intensity of the lighting depends on the number of instruments used, the distance between the instruments and the dancers, and how light is filtered before it reaches the stage. The direction of the instruments and how light is spread over the stage space determine distribution, whereas movement refers to alterations in the qualities of the light. The color of the lighting also requires careful thought and planning. Color is determined by the color of the gel, or **color media,** placed in the instruments. You can use lighting to make some stage areas visible, establish time and place, create a mood, reinforce movement style, provide focus for the audience, organize a composition of related areas onstage, and establish rhythm over a period of time (Yeatman 2003). Lighting can also enhance the overall composition or series of pictures created in choreography.

Chapter 2 contains descriptions of how various forms of computer technology have been used in creating images projected on a backdrop from either front or rear positions. In such cases, you or your lighting designer should take care when positioning and focusing lighting equipment, because light thrown from the instruments could fade or even destroy special effects. It may even be necessary to limit illumination to certain areas of the stage so that projected images can be seen. Colors used for lighting stage areas should also complement the colors used in any special effects or projected images.

Equipment

Among the most common types of lighting equipment are **spotlights, striplights,** and **floodlights** (also called **scoops**). Spotlights can be of two basic types: Fresnel and ellipsoidal. Fresnel spotlights have a fairly short housing and produce soft light; ellipsoidal spotlights have a much longer **housing,** are more focused, and can throw light longer distances. The PAR 64 lighting instrument, also frequently used, produces light that is similar in quality to the effect produced by a Fresnel. The PAR (an acronym for parabolic aluminized reflector**)** has an oval beam of light and can provide good side light. See figure 4.10 for a generic example of a lighting instrument.

Striplights consist of a series of **lamps** set in a long trough; usually every fourth lamp is on the same circuit and is covered with **media** of the same color. Striplights are used in lighting the backdrop, and on small stages they can provide general illumination.

Floodlights, or scoops, have no lens but contain a single lamp in a housing with a large opening. They are also designed to provide general lighting. Because they have no lens, scoops are difficult to control and are best used for lighting large areas in one color.

Figure 4.10 A lighting instrument. The C clamp is at the top of the instrument and attaches it to the pipe. The gel frame is at the front.

Positioning

Bear in mind that some lighting equipment must be burned with the **lamp base** pointed up. Other instruments require the lamp base to be pointed downward, and some lamps can be placed in either a base-up or a base-down position. Check the instructions for proper positioning of instruments.

Your lighting designer will need enough instruments to cover the stage area with overlapping **pools,** or circular areas, of light. Performers cannot be seen when they dance in the dark, so it is paramount that all important stage areas be illuminated. Stanley McCandless was one of the first designers to devise a system for lighting the stage so that the performers appear natural and three dimensional; to achieve these effects he used six pools of light that were 8 to 10 feet in diameter or 2.4 to 3 meters (Yeatman 2003). As a rule, six pools of light are sufficient for general lighting on a small stage (a stage approximately 20 feet wide, or 6 meters). The instruments that create the pools are positioned either in front of and above the stage or to the back or side of the stage. The angle of each beam of light is about 45 degrees vertical to the stage floor so that body shape and form are revealed. This 45-degree angle can be altered to some extent when conditions do not allow for proper location of lighting instruments, but you or your lighting designer will have to judge whether or not the desired effect is achieved. The six pools of light must overlap by about 2 feet (0.6 meter), although more overlapping is better and will ensure that there are no dark spots onstage.

Each of the six pools of light is created by two spotlights, one coming from stage right and the other from stage left. Ellfeldt and Carnes (1971) propose that pool 1, or area 1, receive its illumination from instruments numbered 1 and 4, pool 2 from 2 and 5, and pool 3 from

3 and 6 (see figure 4.11). The lighting instruments used for creating the three downstage areas are either positioned in the **beams** or are attached to a balcony rail located above the audience and in front of the stage. The three upstage areas (pools 4, 5, and 6) receive their illumination from instruments placed on a **pipe** proportionally closer to the performance area above the **apron,** or front of the stage (Ellfeldt and Carnes 1971).

To cover a larger stage, your lighting designer will need to use more instruments to produce more overlapping pools of light. The number of pools used depends on both the number of lighting instruments available and the size of the stage (see figure 4.12). When more pools are used, each pool is also created with two instruments. The main point in using overlapping pools of light is to provide good general illumination onstage. This type of lighting does little, however, to sculpt the body or pull the figure out from the background. Remember that all instruments must be secured according to proper safety regulations.

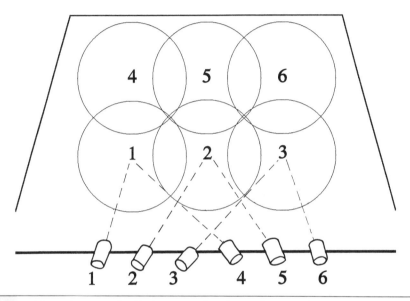

Figure 4.11   The six basic pools of light. Notice that the two beams of light come together from opposite directions and blend to create one pool.

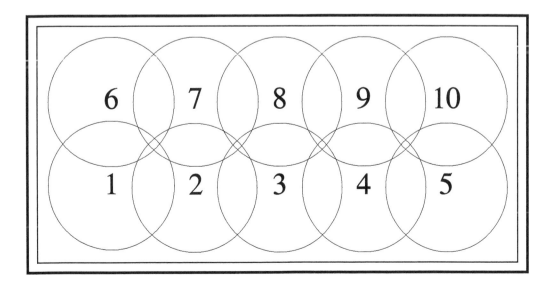

Figure 4.12   More pools of light are needed to cover a larger stage.

You can check for dark spots by having someone walk slowly from one side of the stage to the other. This check is done while all lighting instruments are on and without color media in the instruments. Check for dark spots in both upstage and downstage areas; if dark spots exist, add more lighting instruments or adjust the focus of instruments already in use to create an even effect.

Front lighting has a tendency to flatten the face and body, making illumination from the side important. Dance is a very sculptural art form, and the audience must be able to see the shapes made by the dancers' bodies. The lighting designer uses side lighting to mold and accent the body, particularly movements of the arms and legs (Cunningham 1993). Side lighting also adds depth and form to the total picture.

To create side lighting, put the instruments on **light trees** placed in the wing or other side positions. These instruments are hidden from view by curtains (the legs) and should not be seen by the audience. The type of instruments you or your designer use for side lighting will be determined by the number and variety of instruments available and by the size of the stage. Remember that side lighting should illuminate the entire body of each dancer, not just the head or any other single body part. You'll find that side lighting mounted at a low level gives dancers a lifted quality; side lighting mounted at middle level provides a clean edge to a dancer's form; and high side lighting adds more shadowing and pulls a dancer out from the background. A beam of light from a high side position also goes over the heads of the dancers and cannot be blocked by a performer positioned close to the light source. (See figure 4.13 for an example of the effect created by side lighting.) Dark spots can be filled in with additional instruments located in the front positions already described.

Figure 4.13   Side lighting molds and shapes the body.

Providing lighting from both front and side positions is advantageous, but it may not be possible in certain situations. In such cases, it is advisable to use the basic general light **plot** involving areas, or pools. A good rule is to begin by locating lighting instruments so that dancers can be seen, and then add available instruments as needed to give shape and color to the individual dance compositions.

Backgrounds

In many cases, a cyclorama (or cyc) provides the background for a dance concert. A cyc is a large piece of light-colored material that is suspended from a pipe, or **batten,** upstage of the dancers. It is sometimes curved forward at each end to mask the upstage corners. Lighting instruments throw light on the cyc so that a flood, or **wash,** of light covers the whole cyc from top to bottom. Striplights located in front and above the cyc produce illumination from the top; additional striplights can be laid on the stage floor behind masking to create a wash of light from below. The only problem with the use of masking upstage at floor level is that it creates a dark band at the lower edge of the cyc, making it difficult for the audience to see the dancers' feet. Thus, if possible, it is preferable for the designer to create a smooth wash of light on the cyc with the use of striplights placed at the top of the cyclorama. Scoops can also be used to produce a wash of color over the cyc if necessary.

Sometimes a dark curtain can make an effective background for a dance, provided that enough light is available to illuminate the performers. Frequently when a dark background is used, the audience sees what is known as a **tracer effect,** or **afterimage,** in which it appears as though each dancer produces a trail or stream of light following their movements. If you can integrate this effect into the visual design of the dance, it can enhance your choreography. The tracer effect will also be more visible if the dancers wear light-colored costumes.

Color Gels

Color is created in stage lighting through the use of a color media, also called a gel. Gels are manufactured in many different colors and are made of transparent, nonflammable polyester. Never use cellophane to create colored light, because the lighting instruments can get very hot and cellophane burns. The color media is placed in front of the beam of light and is held in place by the frame located at the front of the lighting instrument (see figure 4.10). The lamp of each instrument gives off white light containing all the colors of the spectrum; when a gel is placed in front of white light, it absorbs all color except for the color of the gel. When a red gel, for example, is put in front of a beam of light, only red light passes through. This effect is called **subtractive lighting.**

Red, green, and blue are considered the **primary colors** in stage lighting. In general, gels in primary colors are not used in lighting dance because they are too intense and absorb too much light. According to Lippincott (1956), gel colors suggested for dance are amber, "bastard" amber, straw, surprise pink, no-color blue, moonlight blue, lavender, red, green, magenta, midnight blue, and frost, which is really not a color. **Secondary colors** can be created from the primary colors through a process known as **additive mixing.** For example, a beam of light filtered through a red gel and a second beam filtered through a green gel create the secondary color amber when the two beams of light are mixed and focused on the same area.

Lighting color should enhance the quality or mood of a piece of choreography. As a rule, blues, greens, and lavenders are cool colors; reds, pinks, and ambers are warm colors. One suggestion is to have warm colors come from one side of the stage and cool colors from the other side; then other colors are blended in to heighten the mood. When in doubt about color, use slightly different colors directed from the right and left sides of a stage area to increase the sculptural molding of the body (Reid 1993). If you do not have sufficient lighting instruments to use opposing warms and cools, use a predominance of one color with some other colors blended in; never use only one color by itself unless you want to achieve a special or unusual effect. For instance, you may want to bathe certain performers in red light to show that they are in or near a fire. In contrast, bathing dancers in blue light could communicate that they are in a very cold or mysterious environment. Also keep in mind that when lighting is done straight on without the appropriate 45-degree angle, it is sometimes better to use a gel that reflects both warm and cool color properties. Such neutral colors are special lavender, surprise pink, and chocolate. The primary colors red, blue, and green plus the secondary color amber can be blended or used alone to create an effective wash on the cyc.

It is essential that you or the designer see all costume colors under the lighting, since colored light changes costume color. Blue light can turn a red costume or red makeup black, whereas red light on a red costume will intensify its shade. Lighting a dance is much easier if you use only one or a few different costume colors in the piece. The best test for lighting color is to have the dancers put on their costumes and move around under the lighting. This should be done during the technical rehearsal.

Green light and green costumes can be particularly difficult to work with. Green lighting creates an otherworldly or strange effect and should be reserved for dances in which such ambience is desired. Pink and amber light can be flattering to the human face but deadly to green costumes.

Special Effects

The designer can augment general lighting through the use of special effects, or **specials.** Specials accentuate specific dancers and can be created by directing a more intense spot of light to the desired area onstage. Specials are usually wired to a different dimmer or electrical source so that each can be operated separately from the general lighting. You can achieve a particularly dramatic effect by positioning a special directly above the performers' heads to produce a pool of light that floods down onto the dancers (see figure 4.14). Performers should dance in specials and position themselves so that they are in the **hot spot,** or the brightest portion of the pool of light. This placement of dancers is especially important during any movement in elevation because the dancer must be illuminated throughout the entire movement sequence.

Another kind of special effect can be created through the use of a gobo, a cutout pattern that throws a patterned pool of light onto the stage or cyc. Patterns of light can enhance a dancer's movement by making small move-

Figure 4.14 Overhead lighting can create a dramatic effect.

ments look larger and by creating an onstage environment. Gobos are used only with ellipsoidal spotlights, in which they are placed at the **gate,** or metal baffle, at the perfect center of the instrument. This placement allows the pattern to be projected without distortion. Gobos can create a star-studded sky, a city scene, or a forest. You can purchase gobos from companies that sell lighting equipment, or you can select them from catalogs containing small black-and-white pictures of the gobo patterns (see appendix A for a list of some of the companies that sell gobos). You can construct gobos by cutting a pattern in sheet metal or even in a pie tin. Never make a gobo out of flammable material.

You can use many other special lighting techniques, such as **back lighting** and cast shadows, to enhance your choreography. In back lighting, the designer places the light source behind the dancers to produce a silhouette. You can easily achieve this effect by lighting the cyc and leaving the remainder of the stage area dark. To cast shadows, the designer positions the light source in a downstage area or areas to create a shadow of each dancer on the cyc or stage floor. The size of the shadow changes as dancers move closer to or farther away from the light source. Sometimes it is necessary to locate the light source on the apron; you or your lighting designer will have to experiment with the placement of lighting instruments to create the desired effect.

You can use a **followspot, black light,** and **strobe** to design additional special effects. The followspot is operated by a technician and is usually located in the light booth at the back of the theater; when used in an informal setting, it is placed above and behind the audience. Followspots are frequently part of musical theater productions or ice skating shows. Black light, also known as ultraviolet light, causes costumes or costume parts that are treated with ultraviolet paint to fluoresce, or glow. For best results, everything else should be black except the treated materials. For example, it is entertaining to see dancers' hats or gloves dance about without being able to see the rest of their bodies. Ultraviolet light also causes costumes that are neon shades of yellow, green, or orange to shine brightly. White costumes appear luminous under black light. A strobe light produces intermittent bursts of light and makes the dancers appear to jump from one pose to the next. Black light and strobe light create powerful visual effects and should be used sparingly. Also, you should know that strobe lights have been linked to epileptic seizures, so it is important to warn the dancers, crew, and audience when such devices will be used in a performance (Reid 1993). People susceptible to seizures should avoid the performance or shield their eyes when the strobe light is used.

As discussed in the postmodern and computer technology sections of chapter 2, you may wish to project slides, videos, or computer-generated images during the performance of your choreography. Images can be projected on the cyc; as dancers move around the stage space they become a part of the projected design. Such images can also be projected from a front position over the dancers' heads or from behind the cyc, so that the performers do not move through the image. Projections can be used as side light as well. When dancers move in and through projected imagery, they should wear simple, light-colored costumes so the images can be seen.

The technical designer must consider the availability of lighting instruments when planning specials. If enough instruments are not available to create the effects described, you can use a few extra pieces of equipment for various specials by changing gel colors or by placing a gobo in an instrument. An assistant can make such changes between dances. You might also need to reposition dancers to accommodate the placement of instruments used for specials.

Light Plot

You can help your lighting designer by putting together a **rudimentary light plot.** The light plot should begin with a general description of each dance, especially the mood or changing moods throughout each piece. The following are other factors to be included in the general light plot:

- A floor plan of the choreography
- Placement of scenery or sets
- Costume colors
- Suggested lighting colors
- Special effects (particularly as they relate to dance movement)

You should supply these suggestions for each dance, since the lighting designer makes the final light plot based on this information. The final plot is a **hanging plot** that includes the following (Ellfeldt and Carnes 1971):

- The placement of each instrument
- The instrument type
- The color with which each instrument is gelled
- The number of the channel connecting each instrument to the control panel or dimmer board

A sample Planning Sheet for Lighting Design is included in appendix B. You can use this form to describe the moods of the dance and the desired visual effects. You may want to design your own forms, but be sure to give the designer a very clear picture of how the lighting should relate to and enhance your choreography. Remember that the hanging plot must be completed before theater rehearsals begin. Your lighting designer will use the plot to determine the placement of each instrument.

If you do not have a lighting designer, you may be able to hire one, or you can enlist the help of a knowledgeable theater student. If you end up doing all of the lighting yourself, keep your design and plot simple. Sometimes a custodian can familiarize you with the location and operation of equipment.

Lighting is supposed to be an integral part of a dance performance; its purpose is to enhance the choreographic illusion, not to detract from it. Lighting changes that occur at unplanned points in a dance are disconcerting for both the performers and the audience. In addition, when the audience notices the lighting rather than the dancing, something is wrong. The designer's job is to blend the two components of dance and lighting together to form a single entity. It is customary to employ very little scenery in dance concerts, so excellence in lighting is essential.

Observing and Responding

EXPERIENCE IN ACTION

1. Look at a video of the same choreography that you viewed in the previous exercises in this chapter. As you play the video, focus on the use of lighting throughout the dance. How does the lighting complement and enhance the mood or message portrayed? Notice the use of area lighting, background lighting, color, and special effects.

2. Can you suggest other possible lighting for use in the work in the preceding exercise? Give a detailed description of how you would use lighting areas, background, color, and special effects.

3. View a second dance on video that is different in tone or feeling than the first dance you viewed. Compare the use of lighting in this choreography to the lighting design used in the first piece.

4. Record all of your observations and ideas in a journal.

Developing Your Skills

LIGHTING THE DANCE

1. Place a light in an otherwise darkened room. (If you are using a table lamp, remove the shade during this exercise.) Notice the area, or pool, of light that surrounds the light source. Watch while a person walks throughout the room. Does the person have a different appearance while moving through various areas of the room? Explain why the visual effect changes as the dancer moves.

2. Continuing the previous exercise, place a second light source in the darkened room. Gradually move one light toward the other until the illumination from the two lights blends together. Then reverse the blended effect by moving the lights apart.

3. Place the two lights so that each reads as a separate lighting area. Watch a person move throughout the space, and again notice the effect produced when the person is positioned near or far from a light source. Can you see the dark areas? What effect do the dark areas have on the person's movements?

4. Use a single light source in a darkened room and ask the person to stand near the light. Experiment with the exact location of the person trying positions above, below, and to the side of the source of illumination. How do the changes in the location affect the appearance of the person? Could such changes in the direction of light be used to complement the mood or message of your choreography? Explain.

5. Place a person in front of first a light-colored and then a dark background. Why is one color more effective as background? Would a light or dark background be most effective for your dance?

6. Return to the light source in a darkened room. Hold a square of color media in front of the light and notice how the light changes color as it passes through the media. (See the list in appendix A for names and addresses of companies that sell color media.)

7. Hold a piece of your costume material under illumination of various colors. Which color media produces the desired effect?

8. Use two lamps to mix light filtered through media of various colors. What colors do you produce by mixing the light?

9. Experiment with back lighting by placing the light source behind the person. Could you use such a silhouette effect in all or part of your choreography?

10. Cut out a pattern in a piece of paper or lightweight cardboard—a snowflake, a cloud, or any other shape. Hold the pattern in front of your light source. The cutout should cast a shadow that outlines the same shape as the original pattern.

11. Project a slide on a bare, light-colored wall. (Photographs of scenery or of abstract paintings work well in this exercise.) Watch while several people move in front of the projection. What effect does the use of the projected image produce? Is it an effect you might use for your dance?

12. Fill out the Planning Sheet for Lighting Design in appendix B. Consider each part of your dance carefully when you use this form.

13. Use the completed Planning Sheet for Lighting Design to design a rudimentary light plot. Include the floor pattern used by each dancer and the placement of props or scenery. Locate each pool of light so that important dance action receives illumination. Be sure to decide on the color media to be used for each pool, and indicate the placement of specials. This light plot could be realistic, based on the type and number of lighting instruments available to you, or it could be the ideal, designed without consideration of the limitations in your situation.

14. In your journal, record your observations and ideas concerning lighting.

15. Mark your master calendar to indicate the date for completing the light plot and for hanging lighting equipment.

Sets and Props

In most instances, choreographers use props and sets in a minimal way, although many of the classical ballets from the 19th century are an exception to this rule. Musicals incorporate more elaborate sets as well. Sets used for jazz and modern dance are more sparse and provide only a suggestion of the performance environment (see figure 3.3, page 86 for an example of such a set). The design of sets and props should begin several months before the concert, although simple sets may take less time to construct.

Dance sets are usually lightweight and fairly flat so that they can be attached to a batten and flown in and out of the stage area. Many sets are made of soft material and can be taken down and rolled up for storage. Dance sets are usually placed upstage to provide a backdrop for the dance, but they can also be used as a border to frame the stage space. Some choreographers have used sculptural sets on which dancers can move or pose (see figure 3.4, page 86). Such sets allow dancers to perform on or between parts of the sculpture. The dancers can also wear or carry props, but the props must contribute to the design or meaning of a dance. You can use props to help create a story, and the props can even be part of the movements.

Observing and Responding

EXPERIENCE IN ACTION

1. Watch a video of a dance that includes sets and props. Describe the choreographer's use of the sets and props. Do you think that they contribute to the effect or meaning of the choreography? Why?

2. View another dance that has a very different tone and in which the choreographer uses sets and props. Compare the contribution or the importance of sets and props in each dance.

Developing Your Skills

SETS AND PROPS

1. Select a prop that you could use during the process of composing a dance (see chapter 1, pages 5 to 6 for a list of suggested props). Experiment with the movement qualities of the prop, and then begin to choreograph phrases that incorporate the prop into the movement design.

2. Select a larger object that could serve as all or a part of your set, such as a bench or a box. Stand or sit on your set, and begin to move. Design several movement phrases in which the set is an integral part of the choreography.

3. If your dance is already complete, visualize how you could incorporate set pieces into the movement design. Decide whether the use of a set would enhance the overall effect.

4. In your journal, record your observations about sets and props.

5. Mark dates on your master calendar for design and execution of sets and props.

Informal Concerts

A stage may not be available in some communities or in some educational institutions. In such cases you can transform a gymnasium or large studio into a relatively professional-looking stage for an **informal concert.** First, however, make sure that an informal performance space has wiring that can accommodate stage lighting equipment. Usually you will need to connect your equipment to a 220-volt outlet to provide adequate power, or you can tie into a breaker box to protect circuits from an overload.

Lighting the Performance Space

You can provide illumination by attaching lighting instruments to **volleyball standards** (poles) used as light trees. The **C clamp** is used for attaching each instrument to the pole, but you should take care to place instruments so that the lamp inside is positioned correctly (see Lighting the Dance, page 115). The standards, with the lighting instruments attached, can supply light from front and, in particular, side positions, but the goal is to come up with a performance area that is evenly illuminated and does not block the audience's sight lines. Experiment with the placement of the lighting equipment and standards until you get the desired effect. Before you attach the lighting instruments to the poles, make sure each standard is stable and heavy enough to counterbalance the heavy instruments. For safety reasons, avoid moving the standards after the instruments are attached. Also check the diameter of the pole on each standard to make sure the clamp on the instrument fits around it.

Framing the Performance Space

You can frame the dance space with **flats** (see figure 4.15). A flat is easy to build: You can construct a wooden frame and then stretch inexpensive muslin over the frame to create the surface of the flat (see figure 4.16). You might have to double-stitch two widths of muslin

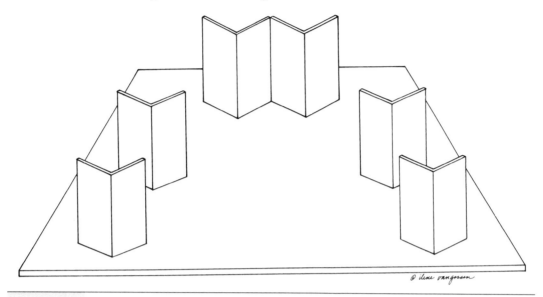

Figure 4.15 Strategically placed flats can create the appearance of a stage in an informal setting such as a gymnasium.

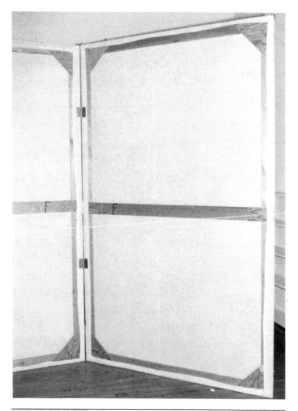

Figure 4.16 Back view of a single flat. Notice how the muslin is folded along the edges of the back of the flat and secured in place with staples.

together to get a piece of material that is wide enough to cover each flat. The muslin is held in place with staples applied with a gun, and the corners of the muslin are folded under and secured with additional staples. The wood used in the flats should be lightweight, because the flats will be moved into and out of the storage area for other performances. Generally, 3.5-by-.75-inch (9-by-2-centimeter) wood cut in desired lengths is recommended for the construction of flats. Use wood that is not warped and that is strong enough to withstand bending after the muslin is stretched in place. The frame for the flats must be high and wide enough to hide dancers from view while they wait to enter the stage area. A single flat should be approximately 5 feet wide and 7 feet high (1.5 by 2 meters).

You can paint the flats once the muslin is stretched over the frames. The paint should be water based, easy to spread, and of a light color. A beige surface is easy to light, but white surfaces appear too stark onstage, and black flats absorb too much light. Beige is a warm color that can be used under many lighting colors and one that won't clash with costume colors.

Construct your flats to be freestanding, since those that need supports take longer to set up. You can make freestanding flats by putting **loose pin hinges** between each flat. You attach two single flats together by inserting a pin into each hinge (see figure 4.17). The flats can stand without added supports when opened at an angle of less than 180 degrees. You can place such flats anywhere in the stage area or use them to outline the space in upstage and stage-right and stage-left positions.

Figure 4.17 A more detailed photo of the back of a flat showing two of the loose pin hinges.

Holding a Lecture-Demonstration

The **lecture-demonstration** is usually presented as the first part of an informal dance concert, although it can be effective as part of a formal concert as well. Your entire production could also be a lecture-demonstration. A lecture-demonstration educates the audience through the combination of spoken text and dance; the dancers perform movements and dances that demonstrate or explain ideas and concepts presented in the lecture. You could structure lecture-demonstrations to illustrate many choreographic concepts—such as style, form, and nonverbal communication—but in each instance you would use movement examples to demonstrate contrasting aspects of each idea. Lecture-demonstrations can be especially helpful for building audiences in communities that are not familiar with dance.

Observing and Responding

EXPERIENCE IN ACTION

1. Attend an informal concert or lecture-demonstration held in your area and take notes on the use of lighting, costuming, accompaniment, and positioning of flats and masking.

2. Do you think each of the elements listed in exercise 1 was used effectively in the performance? For example, did the performance area have adequate illumination and masking? Were entrances and exits effective or distracting? Did the use of music and costumes contribute to the overall effect?

3. Decide whether you would have changed any of the elements in the performance, and note those observations in your journal.

Developing Your Skills

HOLDING AN INFORMAL CONCERT

1. Choose a place in which you could hold an informal dance concert. The space should be free of pillars and large enough to accommodate your choreography.

2. Draw a diagram to indicate placement of flats, lighting, and sound equipment. Make sure that you have enough cabling to connect the lighting instruments to the electrical outlets. On your diagram, show where the dancers will change costumes and how they are to enter and exit the performance area.

3. Plan a schedule of events leading up to the concert. Include dates for the audition, rehearsals, completion of costumes and sound recordings, setup, blocking, and technical run-through.

4. Plan a sample lecture-demonstration by beginning with a dance topic or idea you want to explain to the audience. Write an outline of your text, and then select movement examples that would demonstrate the main points of your outline. Record your ideas for a lecture-demonstration in your journal.

Time to Perform

Any creative endeavor is an exercise in problem solving. One of the challenges is to choose a direction and then to persevere—to make the imagined entity a concrete reality. In dance, more than any of the other arts, there is potential for creating something from nothing—molding movement to fit the forms and images emerging from your mind. The preceding suggestions concerning movement discovery and choreographic craft are offered as a series of steps to guide you, particularly in the early stages of choreographic exploration. Those ideas can assist you with a creative impasse, should one arise, and help you release your creativity.

PRACTICAL APPLICATIONS

CREATE

1. Return to the dance you created in the Create section toward the end of chapter 3. That was the work based on one of the sculptures in figure 1.10, *a* or *b*.
2. Design a costume for your piece, or adapt a costume that is already available.
3. What color lighting would complement your work, and where would you focus pools of light in the performance area?
4. Decide whether you would use any special lighting effects during the performance of your dance.
5. Would you use props or sets in your dance?

PERFORM

1. Perform your dance in the costume you designed and with the props and accompaniment you selected. If possible, experiment with some of the lighting effects you designed as well.
2. Have a friend, preferably someone who is familiar with dance or theater design, watch as you perform your work in costume and with the use of accompaniment, props, or lighting you designed or selected.
3. Videotape the performance of your dance using the same costume, props, accompaniment, and lighting.

REFLECT

1. Have a discussion with your friend about how the use of the costume, accompaniment, props, and lighting affected the performance of your dance.
2. View the video of the performance of your dance.
3. Would you change your use of costume, accompaniment, props, or lighting after discussing your performance with your friend and after viewing the video?
4. Make any desired changes in your use of costume, accompaniment, props, or lighting and perform your dance again. Then make a second video of your dance. Do you think the changes improved the overall effect?

Choreography Challenge

You need to consider costumes, lighting, props, and sets throughout the dance-making process, but it is in the final preparatory steps and rehearsals described in this chapter that all of these elements are actually brought together. In terms of the framework for creating movement and making dances, the integration of costumes, lighting, and sets is usually a final step in the preparation for performance. Sometimes, however, you might still need to circle back through the creative process, discovering new movements, rearranging actions, or making changes in the overall form of your dance. In the following Choreography Challenge, return to the dance you created in the Choreography Challenge at the end of chapter 3. That was the dance based on the inspiration you selected from the list on pages 5 to 7 in chapter 1.

Designing and Constructing Your Costume

- Make a sketch of several possible costumes for your dance. Select one of the costumes you have designed and consult with your costume person, or get some advice on how you can construct the costumes yourself.
- Try your costumes on your dancers to make sure they fit properly. In addition, have your dancers perform some of the movements in your dance in the studio while wearing the costumes.
- Make any necessary changes in the costumes if they restrict the movements of your dancers or cause other problems.

Blocking Your Dance

- Have your dancers move through your entire dance on the stage or in the space in which it will be performed.
- Does your dance fit nicely on the stage or in the space? Do you need to change or rearrange any part of your dance?

Lighting Your Dance

- Think about how you would like to light your dance. Consider the use of color, specials, area lighting, or projected images.
- Decide whether your dance could be enhanced through the use of some form of computer technology.
- Experiment with the various uses of lighting that you have in mind. The easiest way to do this is to have your dancers move through your dance under the lighting you designed and while they are wearing their costumes. This rehearsal will need to stop from time to time as the lighting is set, changes are made, and cues are recorded.
- If time permits, run your entire dance with the music and lighting.

Dress Rehearsal

- Have your dancers perform your dance in full costume and makeup and with the desired lighting. Any accompaniment should be played on the equipment that will be used during the performance.
- Are there any last-minute changes that you need to make? For example, you might have to secure part of a costume or position your dancers so that they perform in the center of the pools of light.

Having successfully moved through all of the preparatory steps, you should now be ready for the real performance.

Appendix A

Choreography Resources

Sources of Music Copyright Information

The following organizations may be able to supply you with information about the copyright holder for your accompaniment.

American Music Center

30 W. 26th Street, Suite 1001
New York, NY 10010
212-366-5260
www.amc.net

American Society of Composers, Authors and Publishers (ASCAP)

One Lincoln Plaza
New York, NY 10023
212-621-6000
www.ascap.org

Broadcast Music Incorporated (BMI)

320 W. 57th Street
New York, NY 10019-3790
212-586-2000
www.bmi.com

European American Music Distributors, LLC

254 West 31st Street
Floor 15
New York, NY 10010
212-461-6940
www.eamdllc.com

New York Public Library for the Performing Arts

Dorothy and Lewis B. Cullman Center
40 Lincoln Center Plaza
New York, NY 10023-7498
212-870-1630
www.nypl.org

Dance Video Sources

Axis Dance Company

1428 Alice Street, Suite 200
Oakland, CA 94612
510-625-0110
www.axisdance.org

British Broadcasting Company (BBC)

BBC Information
PO Box 1922
Glasgow G2 3WT
www.bbc.co.uk

Princeton Book Company/Dance Horizons Videos

P.O. Box 831
Hightstown, NJ 08520
609-426-0602
800-220-7149
www.dancehorizons.com

Dance Notation Bureau

151 West 30th Street, Suite 202
New York, NY 10001
212-564-0985
http://dancenotation.org

Elektra/Nonesuch Dance Collection (Warner Brothers is parent company)

Beverly Hills, CA 90210
www.nonesuch.com/main.html

Hoctor Dance Enterprises

P.O. Box 38
Waldwick, NJ 07463
800-462-8679
www.hoctordance.com

Kultur International Films, Ltd.

195 Highway 36
West Long Branch, NJ 07764-1304
732-229-2343
800-573-3782
www.kultur.com

Madera Cinevideo

311 South Pine, Suite 102
Madera, CA 93637
800-828-8118
www.mcinavideo.qpg.com

Nikolais-Louis Foundation for Dance, Inc.

121 West 20th Street, #2C
New York, NY 10011
646-336-0774
www.nikolaislouis.org

Pyramid Media

P.O. Box 1048\WEB
Santa Monica, CA 90406-1048
310-828-7577
800-421-2304
www.pyramidmedia.com

Ririe-Woodbury Dance Company

138 West Broadway
Salt Lake City, UT 84101
801-297-4213
www.ririewoodbury.com

Video Artists International and VAI Audio

109 Wheeler Avenue
Pleasantville, NY 10570
www.vaimusic.com/index.htm

Dance Floor Companies

Portable floors are available in strips of material similar to linoleum and can be rolled out and taped in place. A portable floor can also be transported from one performance location to another if you decide to go on tour. Many companies sell portable, multipurpose dance floors that can be used for many forms of dance.

American Harlequin Corporation

1531 Glen Avenue
Moorestown, NJ 08057
856-234-5505
800-642-6440
www.harlequinfloors.com

Norcostco

4395 Broadway
Denver, CO 80216
303-620-9734
800-220-6934
www.norcostco.com

Rosco Laboratories

52 Harbor View
Stamford, CT 06902
203-708-8900
800-767-2669
www.rosco.com

Stage Step USA

4701 Bath Street, #46B
Philadelphia, PA 19137
215-636-9000
800-523-0960
www.stagestep.com

Lighting Equipment Manufacturers and Distributors

Altman Stage Lighting Company, Inc.

57 Alexander Street
Yonkers, NY 10701
914-476-7987
800-425-8626
www.altmanltg.com

Cinemills Corporation

2021 Lincoln Street
Burbank, CA 91504
818-843-4560
www.cinemills.com

**Colortran, Inc.
(Leviton is parent company)**

Leviton–NSI Division
P.O. Box 2210
Tualatin, OR 97062
503-404-5500
800-736-6682
www.colortran.com

Olesen Company

19731 Nordhoff Street
Northridge, CA 91324
818-407-7800
800-233-7830
www.hollywoodrentals.com

Rosco Laboratories

52 Harbor View
Stamford, CT 06902
203-708-8900
800-767-2669
www.rosco.com

Strand Lighting, Inc.

6603 Darin Way
Cypress, CA 90630
714-230-8200
www.strandlight.com

Theatrix, Inc.

636 Daniel Shays Highway
Belchertown, MA 01007
413-323-7803
www.theatrix.net

Appendix B

Forms and Checklists

Choreographic Assessment Sheet

Each of the following criteria can be worth 1 or 2 points depending on the total points desired in the scale. You may use fractional points as well. For example, if you think that the choreographer has created a dance that has a sense of form throughout, enter the maximum score for item 1 in the appropriate blank. If a sense of form is intermittent, score a fraction of the points, and give no points for item 1 if the dance has no sense of form or development.

If you find use of points bothersome or intimidating, simply use this form as a guide for describing your comments or suggestions concerning a dance. Other components more compatible with your own choreographic concepts can be substituted for some of the items listed.

Score

1. Overall form: beginning, middle, end   _____

2. Unity, continuity, flow   _____

3. Variety, movement manipulation, sequence, opposition   _____

4. Repetition throughout overall form   _____

5. Development of phrasing   _____

6. Interesting relationship among dancers or articulate and creative use of body shape   _____

7. Use of stage space: blocking, stage area, pathways, awareness of stage space   _____

8. Facings   _____

9. Communication of intent, idea, or feeling, or successful solution of problem   _____

10. Performance, projection, vividness of movement quality   _____

Total points _____

Comments

_____

_____

_____

_____

_____

_____

_____

From S. Minton, 2007, *Choreography: A Basic Approach Using Improvisation, 3rd Edition* (Champaign, IL: Human Kinetics).

Dancer's Audition Form

Name: _____ Audition number: _____

Address: _____

City and zip code: _____

Phone number: _____

Height: _____ Weight: _____

Please list times you will be available for rehearsals. _____

_____

Performance Organization Checklist

☐ Scheduling the audition: _____

☐ Organizing and posting the studio rehearsal schedule: _____

☐ Designing the costumes: _____

☐ Designing the props: _____

☐ Designing the set: _____

☐ Preparing the rudimentary light plot: _____

☐ Collecting information for the printed program: _____

☐ Recording accompaniment: _____

☐ Rehearsal scheduling and posting: _____

☐ Blocking rehearsal: _____

☐ Technical rehearsal: _____

☐ Dress rehearsal: _____

☐ Checking the dance floor: _____

Printed Program Information Sheet

Dance title: _____

Grants or funding sources: _____

Choreographer: _____

Musical artists and composers: _____

Music title: _____

Recording company: _____

Credits (costume designer, props, construction, and so on): _____

Dancers (in alphabetical order): _____

_____

_____

_____

_____

_____

Program notes: _____

Program Supplement
(To be used for collaborative concerts)

Name of institution, group, or school: _____

Contact address and phone: _____

Choreographer's background information: _____

Sample Entry for Printed Program

Mountain Mystery

This dance was made possible through a grant from the Young Foundation.

Choreographer .... Suzanne Jones

Music .... Ralph Limon, "Sunset Song,"
Methods Recording Company

Costume design .... Cecile Dawson

Dancers .... Julie Applebee, Margery Stayer, Alice Whimple

Planning Sheet for Lighting Design

1. How many sections are in your choreography?

   _____

   _____

2. What is the style of your dance? Is it literal, comic, geometric, and so on?

   _____

   _____

3. Briefly describe the story line or action in each section of your dance.

   _____

   _____

4. Describe the costumes and costume colors, and provide samples of the fabric.

   _____

   _____

5. On the rough plan below, describe and show the stage areas to be used in your dance.

   _____

   _____

6. Dance plan:

From S. Minton, 2007, *Choreography: A Basic Approach Using Improvisation, 3rd Edition* (Champaign, IL: Human Kinetics).

a. Outline the placement of any set in the diagram, and then describe how your dancers use it.

_____

_____

b. Use numbers on the diagram to indicate the location of important action in your dance. Then describe how such action can be enhanced with special effects.

_____

_____

c. Briefly describe the action(s) involved for each special.

_____

_____

d. Indicate the mood, quality, or focus to be achieved with each special.

_____

_____

7. Will you be using projections on the cyclorama?

_____

_____

8. Would you like any patterns or gobos?

_____

_____

9. How do you see lighting enhancing your dance? Be specific.

_____

_____

10. How do you want the audience to respond to your dance?

_____

_____

Appendix C

Dance and Technology Web Sites

http://a.parsons.edu/~bkluu/thesis2/01/motion/riverbed.html

This is a site that lists information about dance and technology and people who have worked with dance and technology. There is a still photo of Biped by Merce Cunningham with the digital artwork created by Shelley Eshkar and Paul Kaiser in the background. Links to visuals and brief information about Troika Ranch, Palindrome, David Rokeby, Levin and Lieberman, Myron Krueger, and Caranza are included.

www.charactermotion.com/danceforms

This is the Credo Interactive site for the computer animation program Dance-Forms. The site includes a gallery of still photos or frames of movies in which DanceForms was used in creating the animations. These animation programs have also been used to visually demonstrate Labanotation scores.

www.companyinspace.com/front/cis_fs.htm

This is the site for Company in Space, based in Melbourne, Australia, and codirected by John McCormick and Hellen Sky. This company has pioneered applications of new technologies to movement. There are many still photos of their work; a photo gallery, some of which can be enlarged for better viewing; a list of their works; and information about the motion capture systems, the Gypsy Exoskeleton, and Polhemus magnetic tracking system.

www.cooper.edu/art/ghostcatching/main.html

This is the Cooper Union site for *Ghostcatching,* a virtual dance installation created by dancer Bill T. Jones and digital artists Shelley Eshkar and Paul Kaiser. The site displays multiple still photos from *Ghostcatching.*

www.credo-interactive.com

This is the site for Credo Interactive and the computer animation program DanceForms.

http://cs.sfu.ca/people/Faculty/Calvert/research.html

This site describes work of the Graphics Multimedia Lab at Simon Fraser University. There is also a LifeForms animation clip from D-Symphonies created by Jimmy Gamonet of the Miami City Ballet. A special program is required for playing this clip.

http://dance.arts.uci.edu/lnaugle

This is a site created by Lisa Naugle. It includes information about Naugle as an interactive performer and choreographer for video animations and telematic performances. The site also describes Naugle's research on motion capture, telematics, and interactivity. In addition, there are multiple links to still photos of her dances, many of which can be enlarged for better viewing. If you have trouble reaching the site using this URL, type "Lisa Naugle" in your search engine.

http://dancenotation.org/DNB

This is the site for the Dance Notation Bureau. It shows some of the basic symbols of Labanotation and provides a list of dance notation scores.

http://healthy.uwaterloo.ca/~rsryman

This site is Rhonda Ryman's home page. It describes courses she teaches and her work with LifeForms.

http://homepage.mac.com/davidrokeby/home.html

This site shows photos of and has information about David Rokeby's interactive installations and his Very Nervous System. Video cameras, image processors, computers, synthesizers, and a sound system are used for creating a space in which movements of the body trigger sounds and music. This site also has a list of Rokeby's interactive performances. If you have trouble reaching this site using this URL, just type "David Rokeby" into your search engine.

www.mikeriggsdesigns.com/AVA.html

This site includes a photo gallery of various theater and dance installations designed by Mike Riggs. These projects use unique lighting effects plus motion-capture effects created by Lisa Naugle. If you have trouble reaching this site using the URL listed here, type the whole URL into the box on your search engine.

www.ruf.rice.edu/~orpheus/jobi

This is the site for Johannes Birringer and the Alien Nation Company. It includes Birringer's biography, some action videos of his electronic installations, and some still photos.

www.troikaranch.org

This is the site for the Troika Ranch Digital Theater. It lists company members, performances, works, media and technology, workshops, and a Web salon, which is a chronicle of ways they have made the Web a part of their performances. There are a few photos of their work with special effects created with technology.

Glossary

AB—A simple choreographic form with two sections having two contrasting themes.

ABA—A simple choreographic form with three sections having two contrasting themes, A and B, followed by a repeat of the first theme in the third section. In ABA, the third section may be a shortened version of the original A section.

abstract—A type of dance style that communicates no message. May also refer to the process of presenting the essence of the real thing in the work of art. (The word *geometric* is used in this text in place of the word *abstract* to avoid confusion with the second meaning.)

abstraction—The process of removing, separating from, or condensing. Distilling something to its essence.

accent—An emphasis (stress) on certain musical counts or with specific movements.

additive mixing—The process of producing a new color in stage lighting by mixing beams of light that are different colors from that of the light being created.

aerial dance—A form of dance created in the space above the stage floor through the use of various devices. Can be combined with performers at the stage floor level.

afterimage—A visual sensation occurring after the external stimulus is gone. (Also known as *tracer effect*.)

alignment—The placement of the body's segments in profile one above the other so that the ear, shoulder, hip, knee, and ankle are as close as possible to a straight line that extends at a right angle to the floor.

animation—Causing otherwise lifeless visual images to move or dance.

apron—The front (most downstage area) of the stage.

arabesque—One of the basic ballet poses in which the body is supported on one leg with the other leg extended behind and at a right angle to the support leg. The arms can be held in various positions to create a line from fingertips to toes.

area—A particular extent or portion of the stage space.

artificial perception—Input that can be appended or understood by some form of technology.

assessment—The measurement or evaluation of achievement in relation to a set of criteria. In creative work, a decision is made to stop because the outcome appears successful or unsuccessful.

asymmetrical—Unbalanced; applies to a body shape or grouping of dancers.

audio suit—A technological sensory device worn by a dancer that transmits signals to a computer, enabling the dancer to control the timing and dynamics of the accompaniment, sounds, or other effects.

auditory—Related to the sense of hearing; descriptive of a type of stimulus for movement.

axial—A movement in which the dancer remains in one spot. Bending, stretching, and reaching are axial movements.

back lighting—A light source positioned upstage or behind the performers.

batten—A metal pipe usually located parallel to the proscenium arch of a stage and from which scenery and lighting instruments are hung.

beam—An opening in the ceiling of the theater from which lighting instruments are suspended.

black light—A filtered ultraviolet light source that causes specially treated parts of a dancer's costume to be visible while untreated costume parts are less visible.

blocking—The process of positioning dancers while making a dance; the act of mounting a finished choreography on stage.

broadband—A type of computer service that provides faster communication via the Internet than a dial-up connection.

canon—A choreographic form based on the use of one repeated movement phrase performed by different dancers' beginning the phrase at a specified number of counts apart. The phrases are danced with and against one another.

C clamp—The clamp at the top of a lighting instrument; it attaches the lighting instrument to a pipe, batten, or pole.

chance—A method of choreographic development based on random selection of movement or random organization of actions.

character—The basic style, quality, or feeling of a dance or of a section of a dance. Also refers to a dancer who performs a specific role.

choreographer—One who discovers movement and organizes actions into dances.

choreography—Many sequences of movement that add together to produce a whole dance with a beginning, middle, and conclusion. (Used interchangeably with the term *dance*.)

classical ballet—A dance form that includes the traditional steps, positions, and body carriage that originated before the 20th century; also can refer to a dance piece choreographed before the 20th century.

closure—The act of bringing dance movement to an appropriate ending, as in the conclusion of an improvisation or choreography.

collage—A choreographic form consisting of pieces of movement that are often unrelated but are brought together to create a whole.

collapsing—A use of energy in which a dancer gives in to gravity.

color media—The material used to give color to white light. (Also known as a *gel*.)

combination—A grouping of connected movements usually prepared for presentation during the latter portion of a dance technique class. Students are expected to learn and perform combinations as part of the class.

comic—A style of movement that appears funny, strange, or unusual to the viewer.

composition—A dance or choreography that exists as a whole with a beginning, middle, and end. Term is usually applied to modern dance choreography.

computer graphics—Stationary or moving images created through the use of a computer or programmed electronic device.

computer program—A sequence of instructions enabling a computer to perform a task or series of tasks. (Also known as *software*.)

concert—A program of separate dances organized into a single performance.

conscious—A state of mind in which the person perceives with a degree of controlled thought or critical awareness.

contact improvisation—Spontaneous movement drawn from actions done while relating to the environment or while in contact with another moving body.

continuity—A principle of choreographic form that provides a natural and organized progression of movement phrases so that one phrase flows naturally into or connects to the next.

contrast—The use of different attributes of the elements of movement. For example, high movement contrasts with movement done at a low level; fast movement contrasts with slow actions.

count—A specific beat among a number of underlying beats that make up a sequence of movements or a measure of music.

craft—The technique of organizing movements into a dance and following their discovery through improvisation; the act of designing and shaping a choreography; specific methods or tools used in developing a dance.

cubism—A modern movement in the arts characterized by abstract structure. Cubism fragments visual forms by displaying several aspects of an object at the same time.

cue—The point in a dance at which appropriate changes in lighting or accompaniment need to occur; also can refer to internal or external stimuli that motivate movements.

cyclorama—A plain piece of cloth extending around and above the upstage area to create a feeling of infinite space and to serve as the background for the dancers.

dance—Many sequences of movement that add together to produce a whole. A dance has organization, progression, and development, including a beginning, middle, and end. (Used interchangeably with the term *choreography*.)

Dance Content Standards—Seven criteria developed to determine what every young American should know and be able to do in the discipline of dance. The standards cover the areas of dance skills, choreographic principles and processes, creation and communication of meaning, aesthetic judgment, cultural and historical concepts in dance, dance and health, and the connection between dance and other disciplines.

dance drama—A presentation using movement to express a message or tell a story, usually by showing relationships among the characters. (Also known as a *narrative*.)

dance floor—A portable surface, usually made of a linoleum-like material, that is rolled out on the stage in strips and held in place with tape of the same color as the floor.

dance in the round—An arrangement of movement sequences that produces a whole and that is designed to be viewed from all sides rather than from only the front.

design—The overall organization of a dance, including use of space, time, energy, and shape; a pattern traced in space or on the floor. Also can mean organizing and structuring a piece of choreography.

developmental stage—A degree or level of accomplishment through which a beginning choreographer passes.

dimmer—A device that determines the amount of electricity passed to a lighting instrument, thereby controlling the brightness of that instrument.

direct imagery—The process of mentally visualizing movements before performing them. Direct images are like a mental rehearsal (Overby 1990).

direct pathway—The straight line traced by moving across the floor or by moving a part of the body in space. Not roundabout.

direction—One aspect of the movement element space. In dance, the eight basic directions in which a dancer can move or face the body are forward, backward, the right and left sides, and the four diagonals.

downstage—Movement toward the front of the stage, closer to the audience.

dramatic dance—A choreographic form that tells a story or expresses a message. Similar to a *narrative*.

dresser—A person who helps a performer change costume.

dress rehearsal—The practice session or "run-through" preceding the performance in which the dancers wear their costumes.

dynamics—The interaction of force and time; the loud and soft aspects of music.

electronic music—Accompaniment produced, altered, or reproduced through electronic means and that uses electronic equipment in a creative manner.

element—Any one of the three components of movement—space, time, and energy (also known as *force*). (Shape is sometimes included as a fourth element.)

energy—One of the elements of movement. Energy propels or initiates movement and causes changes in movement or body position. (Used interchangeably with the word *force*.) Six energy qualities are described in this text: sustained, percussive, vibratory, swinging, suspension, and collapse.

ensemble—A group of dancers who perform together.

environment—The surroundings or space in which dance movement takes place. Environments can serve as the motivation for improvised movement.

essence—The fundamental nature of a person or thing.

experiment—To try a variety of movement solutions to solve a specific choreographic problem.

experimental—A type of choreography that uses new movement materials or new concepts of form.

exploration—A process producing spontaneous movement based on suggestions made by a leader. The exploration process is not as in-depth as improvisation.

expressionism—A modern movement in the arts characterized by the desire to depict the subjective emotions and responses of the artist, rather than the appearance of objective reality.

facial expression—A configuration or shaping of features of the face that indicates or projects feeling.

facing—The direction toward which the front of the body is positioned; where one's face is directed.

flat—A wooden frame with muslin stretched over it. Flats provide background and legs (side curtains) in an informal setting.

floodlight—A lighting instrument that has no lens and that casts a broad beam of light. It usually has a metal housing, reflector, and single lamp. (Also referred to as *scoop*.)

floor pattern—A pathway traced on the floor using locomotor movements.

flow—To transmit energy from one part of the body to another; to move a costume in relation to the actions in a dance.

focal point—A place where the audience readily looks onstage or within a group of dancers.

focus—A place where dancers direct their faces and eyes. Also a point of attention for the audience.

follow—To simultaneously copy the movements of another dancer, while facing the same direction as the leader.

followspot—A lighting instrument used to highlight and follow a dancer around the stage or performance area.

force—One of the elements of movement. Force propels or initiates movement, or it causes changes in movement or body position. (Used interchangeably with the word *energy*.)

form—The overall shape, organization, or development of many movement sequences.

framework—A description or suggestion that limits movement materials discovered during exploration or improvisation. Also a diagram depicting the creative movement process in dance.

gate—A metal baffle located just before the focal point in ellipsoidal spotlights. At this point light rays are still converging, and the gate cuts off stray rays to provide a controlled light beam.

gel—The media used to give color to white light. (Used interchangeably with *media*.)

geometric—Descriptive of dances that do not communicate feelings or messages. The emphasis is on movement variation, line, and design. (In this text, the word *abstract* means the same thing.)

global imagery—A suggestion or motivation for movement that is general and directed at the whole body (Hanrahan & Samela 1990).

gobo—A mask placed at the gate of a spotlight to project a pattern by blocking out portions of the light beam.

ground bass—A choreographic form usually providing the movement materials for only part of a dance. In a ground bass, a phrase is repeated throughout while a more complex series of movements is performed by other dancers. The more complex actions play against the simple movements (Lockhart and Pease 1982).

hanging plot—The final form of the light plot indicating type, location, gel color, and circuiting for each lighting instrument used in a concert.

hot spot—The most intense place in a pool of light thrown by a spotlight. For good visibility, a dancer should perform in the hot spot.

house—The area of the theater in which the audience is seated.

housing—The outside portion of a lighting instrument that surrounds other components.

idea—A motif, motivation, or stimulus for movement.

image—A mental picture or body (kinesthetic) feeling.

improvisation—A process producing spontaneous movements stemming from a specific stimulus; a more complete and inner-motivated spontaneous movement experience than exploration.

impulse—A burst of energy greater than what came before or after.

incubation—A stage of the creative process in which the problem is put aside to germinate.

indirect imagery—A motivation for movement that is outside the body. Indirect images are like a metaphor. An example is to move like a feather floating on the breeze (Studd 1983).

indirect pathway—The curved line traced by the whole body as it travels across the floor or by a part of the body in space. Takes a more roundabout route than following a direct pathway.

informal concert—A program of separate dances performed for the public in a setting such as a gymnasium or dance studio rather than on a stage.

inspiration—Anything that has the potential to initiate movement during improvisation. The beginning step in the creative movement framework. (Used interchangeably with *intent*.)

intent—The motivation that stimulates movement.

intelligent stage—A dance performance area equipped with various forms of technology so that a dancer's movements trigger repetitive sounds and visual effects.

interactive—Two-way communication facilitated by computers between dancers and various forms of technology.

Internet—A large computer network linking smaller computer networks throughout the world. Also known as the Net and the Web.

involvement—The process of focusing on movement and body sensations that requires more than a superficial level of attention.

inward focus—The process of paying attention to stimuli that come from within oneself.

isolation—Movements restricted to one area of the body, such as the shoulders, rib cage, or hips. Isolations are prevalent in jazz dance.

jazz—A dance form that developed along with jazz music. Jazz dance has appeal through its energy and variety.

kinesthetic—Pertaining to sensations from the body that relate information about body position, movement, or tension.

kinesthetic imagery—A motivation that describes the body feeling stimulated by the resulting movements.

kinesthetic sense—A mode of receiving information from sense organs that provides information about body position, tension, movement, and so forth.

Labanotation—A system of written symbols used in recording dances. Invented by Rudolf Laban.

lamp—The illuminating device within a lighting instrument.

lamp base—The bottom of the light source within the instrument. All lamps must be burned in the proper position, whether base up or base down.

learning style—The preferred mode of understanding information. Some people are visual, some are auditory, and others are kinesthetic learners.

lecture-demonstration—An informal performance including verbal explanations of dance elements and theories together with movement demonstrations of the theories.

legs—Curtains at the sides of the stage that hide dancers waiting to enter the performance area.

level—One of the aspects of the movement element space. In dance the three basic levels are high, middle, and low.

lighting designer—The person who creates the final, or hanging plot.

light tree—A vertical, freestanding pipe with side arms to which lighting instruments are attached. Light trees are usually placed in the wings behind the legs.

line—A spatial aspect of dance movement; lines are created in space as dancers move, or through the placement of parts of the body. Line can be curved, straight, or a combination of these two.

literal choreography—Choreography that communicates a story or message to the audience.

locomotor—A term used to describe dance movements that move across space.

loose pin hinge—A type of hinge in which the central pin can be easily removed.

lyric—A term describing a movement style characterized by actions that are smooth, calm, and controlled.

manipulation—Varying of movement, particularly in terms of space, time, energy, or shape.

masking—Neutral materials defining the performance area or concealing technical equipment.

master calendar—A block calendar used in organizing a performance. Specific dates for the completion of costumes and other details are indicated on the master calendar.

master tape—The main or original tape recording used in providing accompaniment for a dance concert. (Also can be in the form of a master disc or master sound file on a computer.)

media—The material used to give color to white light. (Used interchangeably with *color media* and *gel*.)

mental image—A picture created in the mind.

metaphor—An image or movement motivation that is likened to an outside object. Collapsing like a pat of melting butter is a metaphor for how to move very slowly to the floor.

meter—The divisions of music into small groups of beats. Usually each grouping has the same number of underlying beats.

mind–body connection—The concept that thoughts in the mind can affect the body, and that changes in the body can alter the mind.

minimalism—A movement form based on the repeated use of the same movement or movement phrase with only slight changes.

mirror—To copy the movements of another person while facing that person.

mixed meter—A metric division of beats in which the separate groupings differ in terms of the number of underlying beats per measure.

mode of sensing—One of the various channels or ways of receiving information from the outside world. Sight and touch are two modes of sensing.

modern ballet—Choreography that maintains elements of traditional ballet but that was created during the 20th century. Many modern ballets are abstract and nonliteral.

modern dance—A performance movement form that developed at the beginning of the 20th century. Modern dance can be contrasted with the other dance forms of ballet, tap, and jazz. Creative work or choreography is an important part of the learning experience in modern dance.

monaural—A sound transmission or recording that has a single transmission path.

motion capture—A technology that enables the movements of a live dancer to be captured on videotape and built or transformed into a series of images through the use of a computer, producing an electronic double of the original performance.

motivation—The starting point or stimulus for creative movement. (Used interchangeably with the word *stimulus*.)

mount—To place and position a dance onstage after the completion of the choreography.

movement ideas—A motivation or stimulus for movement that exists in the mind as a thought or concept.

movement manipulation—A method of changing an action, movement, or phrase so that it looks and feels different. The elements space, time, energy, and shape can be used to manipulate movement.

movement potential—The range or degree of motion possible in a joint of the body.

narrative—A choreographic form that tells a story. Also known as a *dance drama.*

negative space—Space surrounding parts of a dancer's body or between two or more dancers. Negative space is part of the overall visual design of choreography, including the space between props, sets, and the stage environment.

nonliteral choreography—Choreography that emphasizes movement manipulation and design without the intent of telling a story. Nonliteral works communicate directly through movement and need no translation.

nontraditional—Choreography created with experimental rather than established methods and forms.

nonverbal communication—Sending a message without the use of words.

observe—To notice or view with attention in order to learn something. One of the thinking tools used by creative people.

opposition—The act of moving or facing the body in a different direction from the movement direction or facing used by another dancer.

optical suit—A technological sensory device worn by a dancer that transmits signals to a computer, enabling the dancer to control accompanying images and video projections.

order—The sequencing and organization of movements, phrases, and themes in a dance.

organic—Pertaining to a dance or sequence of movements that has an interrelationship of parts similar to the form or organization of parts in nature.

overall development—The form or development of an entire sequence of movements as it progresses from beginning to end. (Also known as *overall shape.*)

pantomime—A nonverbal but realistic use of action and gesture as a means of expression. Dance is more abstract than pantomime.

path or pathway—The designs traced on the floor as a dancer travels across space; the designs traced in the air as a dancer moves various body parts.

pattern—The organization of movements into recognizable relationships. Also refers to the organization of sounds into identifiable groupings.

pedestrian—Descriptive of movements from daily life that are not traditionally done in dance, such as sitting, standing, eating, or typing.

perceiving—Achieving an awareness or understanding based on sensory information.

percussive—Use of energy that is powerful and explosive.

phrase—The smallest and simplest unit of dance form. The movements that accompany the inhalation and exhalation of one breath would make up a movement phrase.

phrasing—The building block of dance form. In music, it is a melodic building block equivalent to parts of a complete sentence in language.

pipe—A long, cylindrical piece of metal usually suspended parallel to the proscenium arch of the stage and from which scenery and lighting instruments are hung.

pitch—The high and low aspects of music as determined by the frequency of sound waves.

plot—A drawing showing the location of each lighting instrument used in a concert in relation to the physical structure of the theater. May also refer to a general description of lighting changes throughout a piece of choreography.

pool—A circle of light thrown onstage by a lighting instrument. Most pools are actually not a perfect circle because of the location of the lighting instrument and the angle at which the beam of light hits the stage. (Theatrical technique recommends the use of two instruments focused to create one pool of light.)

postmodern dance—A form of modern dance that evolved in the 1960s and 1970s in which choreographers experimented with concepts and forms that challenged more traditional ideas.

potential—The number or kinds of movements possible in each of the joints of the body.

preparation—The actions or processes that one goes through to get ready to do creative work.

primary colors—The three most basic colors in stage lighting—red, green, and blue. These colors produce white light when all three are mixed together.

project—To throw one's energy out toward the audience; to make movement onstage more visible or alive; or to be exact in terms of movement expression.

prop—An object that is separate from the dancer's costume but that is a part of the action or spatial design in a choreography or that contributes to the meaning of a dance.

proscenium—The arch that frames the stage area and through which the audience views a performance in traditional theater settings.

pulse—The underlying and steady beat in dance or music. The pulse is divided into groupings, or measures, with a specific number of beats per measure; a rhythmic pattern is created over and in relation to the pulse.

quality—Movement characteristics determined by the specific use of energy. Sustained, percussive, and vibratory are movement qualities.

realism—A movement in the arts characterized by a faithful representation of nature or life without distortion or idealization.

repetition—A principle of choreographic form based on using movements or phrases again in a work. Repetition adds closure because the audience feels familiar and more involved with repeated movements.

response—Feelings that result from involvement with an inspiration. Part of the framework of creative movement.

rhythm—A structure of patterned movement through time.

rhythmic pattern—The organization of movements or sounds into recognizable groupings or relationships. A rhythmic pattern is created by moving more slowly or faster than the underlying pulse or by leaving silences in the movement.

rondo—A choreographic form with many different sections. There is a return to the original theme in alternation with contrasting sections. It can be described as ABACADAEAFA.

rudimentary light plot—A general description of a dance as related to any and all possible lighting to be used in that dance. The hanging plot is developed from this description.

scoop—A lighting instrument that contains no lens and is used primarily to throw a wash of light on the cyclorama. (Also known as *floodlight*.)

secondary colors—The colors in stage lighting produced by mixing beams of light of two primary colors. The secondary colors are cyan, magenta, and amber.

section—Part of a dance smaller than the whole that contains many phrases.

semblance—An object or work of art that has the appearance of or that resembles something else. An abstraction is the semblance of the real thing.

sensory mode—A method of receiving environmental stimuli by means of the various human sense organs, such as the eyes and ears.

sequence—A series of movements longer than a phrase but much shorter than a section of a dance; similar to a combination. Also refers to the ordering of movements and phrases in a choreography.

sequential—An arrangement of movements or phrases producing an overlapping effect in time.

shape—An interrelated arrangement of body parts of one dancer; the visible makeup or molding of the body parts of a single dancer; the overall visible appearance of a group of dancers. Also the overall development or form of a dance. When used as a verb, *shape* means to give form and development to choreography.

sight lines—Lines of visibility between the audience and the stage.

silence—An absence of movement in which dancers hold a position.

size—One of the aspects of the movement element space. Size can vary from the smallest possible performance of a movement to the largest.

space—One of the elements of movement. The dancer moves in and through space. Dance movement takes up space, and a dance is performed in a space. Direction, level, size, focus, and pathway are the aspects of space described in this text. An altered use of the aspects allows the choreographer to use space in different ways.

spatial design—A pattern traced in space with the whole body or a part of the body.

special—The use of lighting onstage to draw attention to a dancer or create a particular feeling. (Used interchangeably with the term *special effect*.)

specific imagery—A motivation for movement that creates a mental picture or a body feeling and is directed at one part of the body (Hanrahan & Samela 1990).

spotlight—Any of a number of types of lighting instruments containing a lens for controlling or condensing a beam of light.

stage left—A direction indicating movement to the performer's left side while that performer is facing the audience.

stage right—A direction indicating movement to the performer's right side while that performer is facing the audience.

stage space—The stage area in which a performance usually takes place. On a traditional stage, the space is framed by the proscenium.

step—A codified, or set, movement in dance that has a specific name.

stereo—Involving the use of separated microphones and two transmission channels to achieve the sound separation of live hearing.

stimulus—The starting point or incentive for creative movement. (Used interchangeably with the word *motivation*.)

striplight—A lighting instrument consisting of a series of lamps usually mounted in a trough and used for general illumination.

strobe—A lighting device that gives off a fast series of short flashes and appears to freeze the action onstage.

structured improvisation—Spontaneous movement based on predetermined rules or within a predetermined framework.

study—A short dance having a beginning, middle, and end and that deals with only one or a few aspects of choreographic craft.

style—A personal or characteristic manner of moving or choreographing. In both dance and music, style can refer to the time period in which the work originated, the specific developmental procedures used, or the cultural context of the work.

subconscious—A term describing a state of mind in which information or ideas exist below the threshold of conscious awareness.

subject matter—The theme or ideas dealt with in a choreography.

subtractive lighting—A lighting technique that involves placing a color media in front of a beam of light to filter out all light colors except those in the media.

suite—A choreographic form with a moderate first section, a slow second section, and a lively third section.

surrealism—A modern movement in the arts and literature characterized by the representation of dreams or irrational and unusual arrangement of materials.

suspended—A term that describes a use of energy that gives a feeling of stopping temporarily or hovering in midair.

suspended floor—A floor of wooden slat construction that gives with and cushions dancers' movements, particularly movements in which dancers land from elevation.

sustained—A use of energy that is slow, smooth, and controlled.

swinging—A use of energy that traces an arc in space. In a swing, the dancer must relax and give in to gravity on the downward part of the arc and apply energy during the upward action.

symmetrical—A visually balanced body shape or grouping of dancers.

syncopation—Placement of accents where they usually do not occur in the metric organization of both music and movement.

synthesizer—A computerized console or piece of equipment used in creating or modifying sounds, usually those of musical instruments.

tableau—A section of a dance in which different movements are performed simultaneously in the same stage space.

tactile—Related to the sense of touch; a type of stimulus for movement.

technical rehearsal—A performance "run-through" during which lighting cues are set in relation to dance movement and the accompanying music.

technique—The learning of movement skills; the ability to use specific methods to create a dance.

technique class—A dance class that focuses on the development of movement skills such as alignment, balance, and coordination. There are many styles and forms of dance technique.

technology—Electronic devices created by engineers or scientists that have changed the dance-making process as it existed before the latter part of the 20th century.

teleperformance—A choreography in which the dancers simultaneously perform in different locations but are connected in a single performance because their images are transmitted across locations via the Internet.

tempo—The speed of movement as it progresses faster, more slowly, or on a pulse beat.

texture—The density or sparseness of a piece of music. Can also be used to describe dance movement.

theme—One or several movement phrases that fit together and are developed from the same idea or intent. Can also mean the basic idea of a whole dance.

theme and variations—A choreographic form developed in which the fundamental idea, or theme, is repeated in altered form or accompanied in a different manner.

time—One of the elements of movement. A choreography develops a form through time. The aspects of time discussed in this book are movement speed, accents, silences, and rhythm. Altering the aspects of time creates changes in a dance.

timing—The rate of speed at which movement is performed, particularly with reference to the underlying beat.

tone—The quality or feeling in movements. The quality, pitch, or modulation of a musical sound.

tracer effect— A visual sensation occurring after the external stimulus is gone. (Also known as *afterimage*.)

transition—An aspect of choreographic form that provides a bridge from one phrase of movement into the next or between sections of choreography. Transitions should fit with dance movements and not be noticeable.

transform—To change appearance, structure, or form. One of the thinking tools used by creative people.

unison—Movement exactly the same as other movements performed by a group.

unitard—A one-piece, close-fitting dance costume that covers the entire body, including the legs. Unitards may or may not have sleeves.

unity—A principle of choreographic form in which phrases fit together. Each phrase is important to the whole.

upstage—A term indicating movement toward the back of the stage, away from the audience.

variety—A principle of choreographic form that involves sufficient variation of movement to keep the audience's interest while still maintaining unity of the whole.

vibratory—Use of energy that involves shaking or trembling actions.

virtual dancer—A dancing image created through the use of computer software and hardware.

virtual entity—The illusion that the audience sees when viewing a dance. The visual apparition is different from the physical moving bodies of the dancers. It encompasses elements that do not exist in physical reality but are created artistically by the choreographer.

visual—Related to the sense of sight; descriptive of a type of stimulus for movement.

visual image—A motivation for movement that is like a picture in the mind (Paivio 1971).

visualize—To see or form an image in the mind.

volleyball standards—Metal poles with large, heavy base to which a volleyball net is attached.

wash—An even blending of light beams from separate instruments; especially an even flooding of light to cover the cyclorama.

wing—The area at the sides of the stage.

References and Resources

Abeling, R., and E. Ruskin. 1998. Music and sound. In J. Schlaich and B. Dupont (Eds.), *Dance: The art of production*. 3rd ed., Hightstown, NJ: Princeton Books.

Anderson, J. 1997. *Art without boundaries: The world of modern dance*. Iowa City: University of Iowa Press.

Banes, S. 2001. Choreographic methods of the Judson Dance Theater. In A. Dils and A.C. Albright (Eds.), *Moving history/dancing cultures: A dance history reader*. Middletown, CT: Wesleyan University Press.

Banes, S. 1993. *Democracy's body: Judson Dance Theater, 1962-1964*. Durham, NC: Duke University.

Bejarano, J. 2002. This speaking body: The process and the product. *Colorado Dance Alliance News* 21 (3): 4.

Birringer, J. 2003 and 2004. Dance and interactivity. *Dance Research Journal* 35 (2), 36 (1): 88-111.

Birringer, J. 2002. Dance and media technologies. *Performing Arts Journal* 70 (1): 84-93.

Blom, L.A., and L.T. Chaplin. 1982. *The intimate act of choreography*. Pittsburgh: University of Pittsburgh Press.

Charlip, R. 1992. Composing by chance. In R. Kostelanetz (Ed.), *Merce Cunningham: Dancing in space and time*, Pennington, NJ: A Cappella.

Csikszentmihalyi, M. 1997. *Creativity: Flow and the psychology of discovery and invention*. New York: Harper Perennial.

Cunningham, G. 1993. *Stage lighting revealed: A design and execution handbook*. Cincinnati: Betterway.

Dilley, B. 1981. Notes from improvisation, open structures. Boulder, CO: Naropa Institute.

Dils, A. 2002. The ghost in the machine: Merce Cunningham and Bill T. Jones. *Performing Arts Journal* 70 (1): 94-104.

Ellfeldt, L. 1967. *A primer for choreographers*. Palo Alto, CA: National Press.

Ellfeldt, L., and E. Carnes. 1971. *Dance production handbook or later is too late*. Palo Alto, CA: National Press.

Foster, S.L. 2001. Simply (?) the doing of it, like two arms going round and round. In A. Dils and A.C. Albright (Eds.), *Moving history/dancing cultures: A dance history reader*. Middeltown, CT: Wesleyan University Press.

Fox, I, R. Ryman, and T. Calvert. 2002. Building bridges: From notation to animation. In H. Scheff and R. Bootz, *Dance: A living legacy of building bridges*. Presentation at annual NDEO Conference, Providence, RI.

Gray, J.A. 1989. *Dance instruction: Science applied to the art of movement.* Champaign, IL: Human Kinetics.

Hanrahan, C., and J.H. Salmela. 1990. Dance images—Do they really work or are we just imagining things? *Journal of Physical Education, Recreation and Dance* 61(2): 18-21.

Hanstein, P. Summer 1980. Notes from improvisation workshop. Denton, TX: Texas Woman's University.

Hawkins, A. 1988. *Creating through dance.* Princeton, NJ: Princeton.

Hayes, E. 1955. *Dance composition and production.* New York: Barnes.

Hodges, M. 1995. Computers and dance. *Technology Review* 98 (1): 20-22.

Horst, L., and C. Russell. [1963] 1987. *Modern dance forms.* Princeton, NJ: Princeton Books.

Humphrey, D. [1959] 1987. *The art of making dances.* Pennington, NJ: Princeton Books.

Jackson, M. 1999. Dancing in the fast lane: Art and technology make slightly uneasy partners. *Technology Review* 102 (3): 92-95.

Jacobsen, M.E. 1999. *The gifted adult: A revolutionary guide for liberating everyday genius.* New York: Ballantine/Random House.

Kaplan, R. 2002. *Rhythmic training for dancers: An interactive guide to music for dancers.* Champaign, IL: Human Kinetics.

Knaster, M. 1996. *Discovering the body's wisdom.* New York: Bantam.

Langer, S. 1957. *Problems of art.* New York: Scribner.

Lavender, L. 1996. *Dancers talking dance: Critical evaluation in the choreography class.* Champaign, IL: Human Kinetics.

Lippincott, G., ed. 1956. *Dance production.* Washington, DC: American Association for Health, Physical Education and Recreation.

Lockhart, A.S. and E. E. Pease. 1982. *Modern Dance: Building and teaching lessons.* Dubuque, IA: Wm. C. Brown.

Maisel, E. 1995. *Fearless creating: A step-by-step guide to starting and completing your work of art.* New York: Tarcher/Putnam.

Marshall, L. 2002. *The body speaks: Performance and expression.* New York: Palgrave Macmillan.

McDonagh, D. 1990. *The rise and fall and rise of modern dance.* Pennington, NJ: A Cappella.

Minton, S. Submitted for publication. *Moving, dancing and learning.*

National Dance Association. 1996. *National standards for dance education: What every young American should know and be able to do in dance.* Reston, VA: Music Educators National Conference.

Naugle, L.M. 1998. Technique/technology/technique. *Dance Research Journal* 30 (1): 13-15.

Naugle, L.M. 2002. Distributed choreography: A video-conferencing environment. *Performing Arts Journal* 71 (1): 56-62.

Overby, L.Y. 1990. The use of imagery by dance teachers—development and implementation of two research instruments. *Journal of Physical Education, Recreation and Dance* 61 (2): 24-27.

Paivio, A. 1971. *Imagery and verbal processes.* New York: Holt, Rinehart & Winston.

Popat, S. 2002. The TRIAD Project: Using Internet communications to challenge students' understandings of choreography. *Research in Dance Education* 3 (1): 21-34.

Povall, R. 1998. Dance and technology: Technology is with us. *Dance Research Journal* 30 (1): 1-4.

Reid, F. 1993. *Discovering stage lighting.* Oxford: Focal Press/Butterworth-Heinemann.

Reynolds, N., and M. McCormick. 2003. *No fixed points: Dance in the twentieth century.* New Haven, CT: Yale University Press.

Robertson, D. 2000. Basic progressive relaxation script. Available at www.ukhypnosis. com/ProgRela.htm.

Root-Bernstein, R., and M. Root-Bernstein. 1999. *Sparks of genius: The 13 thinking tools of the world's most creative people.* Boston: Houghton Mifflin.

Rossman, M., and D. Bresler. 2004. What is interactive guided imagery? Available at www. academyforguidedimagery.com/whatis.php.

Rugg, H. 1963. *Imagination.* New York: Harper & Row.

Samuels, M.D., and H. Bennett. 1973. *The well body book.* New York: Random House/ Bookworks.

Schiphorst, T. 1992. LifeForms: Design tools for choreography. In A.W. Smith (Ed.), *Proceedings of Dance and Technology I: Moving toward the Future.* Westerville, OH: Fullhouse.

Schneer, G. 1994. *Movement improvisation: In the words of a teacher and her students.* Champaign, IL: Human Kinetics.

Schrader, C.A. 2005. *A sense of dance: Exploring your movement potential.* 2nd ed. Champaign, IL: Human Kinetics.

Studd, K. 1983. Ideokinesis, mental rehearsal and relaxation applied to dance technique. Master's thesis. University of Oregon, Eugene.

Swift, C.I. 2004. *Introduction to stage lighting: The fundamentals of theatre lighting design.* Colorado Springs: Meriwether.

Taylor, J., and C. Taylor. 1995. *Psychology of dance.* Champaign, IL: Human Kinetics.

Teck, L. 1994. *Ear training for the body: A dancer's guide to music.* Pennington, NJ: Princeton Books.

Topaz, M. 1995. Whose right: How to get the rights to choreograph copyrighted music. *Dance Magazine* 69 (5): 52-55.

Turner, M. 1971. *New dance.* Pittsburgh: University of Pittsburgh Press.

Ulrich, D. 2002. *The widening stream: The seven stages of creativity.* Hillsboro, OR: Beyond Words.

Wechsler, R. 1998. Computers and dance: Back to the future. *Dance Research Journal* 30 (1): 4-10.

Yeatman, R. 2003. As a fish lives in water, a dancer lives in light. In M.H. Nadel and M.R. Strauss (Eds.), *The dance experience: Insights into history, culture and creativity.* 2nd ed. Hightstown, NJ: Princeton Books.

Index

Note: The letters *f* and *t* after page numbers indicate figures and tables, respectively.

About the Author

Photo courtesy of Glamour Shots, Park Meadows Mall. Glamour Shots has turned into a lifestyle portrait studio, for business shots to families and all ages.

Sandra Cerny Minton, PhD, was professor and dance director at the University of Northern Colorado from 1972 to 1998. She is now a dance specialist in the public schools. Her other books include *Modern Dance: Body & Mind* (1991), *Dance Mind & Body* (2003), and *Preventing Dance Injuries* (2005), on which she served as a coeditor. Dr. Minton's research has focused on dance teachers' behaviors, the role of imagery in teaching dance, and the effects of dance on students' self-esteem and creative thinking. This research has been published in several juried journals. In 1999, Dr. Minton was selected as the National Dance Association Artist/Scholar, and in 2001 she taught in Finland as a Fulbright Scholar.